HOW TO COACH
A SOCCER TEAM

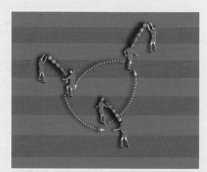

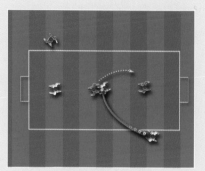

HOW TO COACH
A SOCCER TEAM

Professional Advice on Training Plans, Skill Drills, and Tactical Analysis

Tony Carr

Foreword by Rio Ferdinand

Sterling Publishing Co., Inc.
New York

PUBLISHER'S NOTES

Gender: Throughout the book individual players have been referred to as "he." This is simply for convenience and in no way reflects an opinion that soccer is a male-only game.

Safety and Equipment: Coaches should take care to follow manufacturers' instructions when setting up any training equipment. In particular, portable goals should always be properly erected and anchored firmly to the ground.

Physical exertion: Coaches should be aware that, contrary to traditional wisdom, players can be worked too hard. Prolonged sessions, particularly those involving plyometric exercises, should be kept short and tailored to meet the needs and abilities of the players.

Library of Congress Cataloging-in-Publication Date Available

10 9 8 7 6 5 4 3 2

Published in 2006 by Sterling Publishing Co., Inc.
387 Park Avenue South, New York, NY 10016

First published by Hamlyn, a division of Octopus Publishing
Group Limited, 2–4 Heron Quays, London, England, E14 4JP
© 2005 by Octopus Publishing Group Limited

Distributed in Canada by Sterling Publishing
c/o Canadian Manda Group, 165 Dufferin Street
Toronto, Ontario, Canada M6K 3H6

Sterling ISBN-13: 978-1-4027-2984-3
          ISBN-10: 1-4027-2984-7

For information about custom editions, special sales, premium and
corporate purchases, please contact Sterling Special Sales
Department at 800-805-5489 or specialsales@sterlingpub.com.

CONTENTS

FOREWORD

Natural ability, hunger for the game and success, and plain hard work, are what make good soccer players. Good soccer players in well-organized teams win matches and championships. And it's inspiring coaches that help get them there.

There's not much a coach can do, however experienced and competent, if soccer ability is wholly absent, but it's amazing what can be done with even modest talent—if the other qualities are available.

Hunger for the game? Playing at under-14 level for Blackheath District team I was scouted by West Ham's Frank Lampard (senior) and joined their youth Academy. It meant three bus and two train rides from Peckham in the south of London to get to the Chadwell Heath training ground in the east of London, three times a week. That was two and half hours each way, after school. I never got to enjoy those journeys or, as it happens, much of my time in the youth set up at the club—at first; but a few months in, a combination of the sheer quality of the training, the club's ethos and history, and learning to play soccer the "West Ham way" all began to make sense and add up to something I would relish. Apart from cleaning Mr. Redknapp's boots, that is.

A couple of years later and I was regularly training under the all-seeing eyes of Tony Carr, head of the Academy. To be honest, at the age of sixteen, I was fairly sure that Tony had made his mind up about me as a player and was not much of a fan! It wasn't until the last game of the season, when I played maybe my best game for months, that I realized that Tony was simply being the professional coach he is and setting demanding standards. He knew, before I did, that I should be playing as a central defender rather than in midfield and could, and should, have a career as a soccer player at the top level.

So, at the beginning of the next season I had signed for the Club and the rest, as they say, is history. Actually the history bit is too much of a simplification. In soccer, as in life, nothing is certain, and that's why hard work is the third leg of the stool. For a soccer player it means training and practice and practice and more practice.

It doesn't matter how much talent you've got, you can always keep on improving—I've seen Sir Alex Ferguson send out for a shepherd's crook to get David Beckham off the training field—but you often need qualified help to see a new and better way of doing things. Soccer is essentially a simple game, but the techniques and skills needed to play the game well have to be ingrained through endless repetition.

Tony was always brilliant at reducing the game to its vital components—movement, control, passing—and designing drills and games that would hone each of them; just as importantly, he paced and varied our training so it was always both demanding and fun.

I am fortunate enough to play the game at the most senior level, but I still rely on the drills and conditioned games I first experienced when working with Tony more than ten years ago. You could do far worse than spend time with Mr. Carr through the pages of this book and apply one of the very best youth coach's ideas, methods and drills to your players and team. Then watch them improve!

Rio Ferdinand
Manchester United and England

INTRODUCTION

When I was first asked by my publisher to write a new book on soccer coaching, my initial reaction was what possibly can be written that is either new or has not been adequately covered before?

After giving the prospect some thought, I came to the conclusion that with so many coaches, teachers and those charged with the development of young players constantly searching for advice about, and fresh direction for, their day-to-day coaching, looking for new stimuli, new ideas or help in ordering their own ideas and thoughts about organizing successful training sessions, it was time to try and put together a book of the hundred or so drills and practices that I have developed over the last thirty years. Drills and practices that I use at West Ham to develop players from their earliest days at the Academy all the way through their careers as senior internationals.

In my position as the manager of West Ham United Academy, I am well placed to examine the constant developments that are taking place in coaching and the management of young players. These days young players are better equipped than ever to deal with the physical and technical demands the game places upon them, and it is down to the hard work and professionalism of amateur coaches, who make sure that young players coming to us, and other clubs around the country, are both willing and able to absorb the training a soccer academy can give them.

At West Ham United, we are justly proud of our youth set-up and it is a testimony to the coaching staff at the Academy that we have produced several generations of very fine players, many of whom have earned international honors, including, most recently, Rio Ferdinand, Joe Cole, Michael Carrick, Jermain Defoe, Glen Johnson and Frank Lampard. The experience of working with players like these on a day-to-day basis is the reason for writing this book—it is a distillation of the hours we spend on the training field.

This book shows you a way to organize your coaching, how to prioritize your topics, and link them to the needs of your team. It stresses the importance of constant practice of the basic skills and techniques of the game by your players, no matter how experienced they are— repetition becomes permanent.

Any book alone will not make you a good coach—that takes years of experience, watching and listening to others and a good deal of trial and error—however, a great deal of thought has gone into the structure, layout and design of this book and I hope, when combined with your own knowledge and enthusiasm, it will help you try out new ideas and increase your understanding of the game. Coaches should be adding to their players' natural game and in promoting simple, straightforward principles, your players should move and pass more intelligently.

One element of the book that is, I believe, genuinely new is Solving Problems. Designed to help you analyze match situations and identify the causes of the problems (many of them quite common) that may possibly be undermining your team's results, it should offer a diagnostic tool and supply you with a logical way to improve things on the training ground. I have tried to give you a range of solutions linked to the drills and technical practices in the book. Hopefully your players and the team's results will improve as a consequence!

One other point I would like to stress: women's soccer is growing rapidly in size and stature and the drills, practices and games discussed in this book are every bit as relevant to girls as they are to boys, although for simplicity's sake, and to avoid a repetitious and clumsy use of he/she and his/her, I have referred to players as "he" throughout.

I do hope you enjoy reading the book and that it helps you to become a better coach.

Tony Carr
Manager, West Ham United Academy, London

1

GETTING ORGANIZED

Soccer is both a beautiful and simple game. The beauty lies in the artistry and athleticism of the players who master its demands, and the simplicity is evident in its direct, uncomplicated aim—to put the ball in the opponent's goal.

The game requires players to possess a range of skills and techniques as well as good levels of mobility and physical fitness; it is the coach's job to break down the game into its most simple components, to analyze and articulate the required techniques and devise drills and practices that, building on natural ability, will develop a player's game and a team's performance.

Coaching well is a challenge and carries a significant responsibility. Anyone with any serious aspirations to coach regularly should visit their national soccer association website and enroll in their training programs.

This is a book of coaching ideas which few, I suspect, will read from cover to cover, but it is organized in way that reflects how a season in charge of a team might progress and it begins with advice about getting organized for your first and subsequent training sessions.

THE FIRST SESSION

Coaching is hard work, and the results that you and your squad accomplish will be only as good as the preparation and effort you put into the training sessions. Being clear about what you want to achieve during a forthcoming season and having a plan to get there is vital; a great deal can be done if the very first session sets the standards for what is to come.

First impressions

First impressions count, and it's important that the coach looks and behaves the part from the outset.

Effective coaching means having access to adequate equipment and properly prepared playing areas for each training session. It is foolish, for example, for the coach to march onto a damp field and try to kick a ball wearing sneakers and ending up on his backside! Do not try to demonstrate techniques you are not competent at.

Always be punctual, prepared, focused and enthusiastic and your squad will treat these values as the norm.

Equipment

This book anticipates that you will have access to a full-sized field and the following equipment:
• a set of cones (packs of 50 are ideal) • 12 (or more) poles • sufficient balls—at least one between two players, preferably a ball for every player (Note: you don't need top-level match balls for training. Use size 4 balls for players aged up to 13 and size 5 for 14+) • small-sized goals • mannequins (a stand-in to represent a defender) • colored bibs

Finally, although the coach may prefer to give verbal commands, a whistle is necessary, particularly when acting as referee in small-sided games.

You should note that the laws of the game now make it compulsory for all players to wear shin pads during matches. It's not just against the rules for players to play without pads; it flies in the face of common sense.

Places to train and safety

If you train indoors make sure that there are no benches or other hazards present at the edge of the training area; everything must be stacked away safely. When practicing indoors, plan to use drills that do not encourage too much player contact, and set the condition for games and drills that insist that the ball is always kept below head height if the indoor hall has a low ceiling

During outdoor sessions, make absolutely sure that mobile goals are securely fixed to the ground with weights or by pinning and cannot possibly topple over.

Ensure there are no hazards, for example lawnmowers or benches, too close to the playing area and that the field is clear of loose balls and as free as possible from potholes.

No child should ever be asked to retrieve a ball from a river, canal or lake.

It is highly advisable that the coach or one of his colleagues is formally trained in first aid.

The governing bodies of the game stipulate that for players less than 12 years of age, games should be played 8 vs. 8 on a 60 x 40 yards (55 x 36m) field with smaller goals. 12–14 year-olds can play 11 vs. 11 but with smaller-sized goals, and at 14+ everything can be full-sized.

All coaches planning to take charge of a squad containing under-18-year-olds must check with their local soccer association about the requirements that have been set in connection with working with children. In the United Kingdom and in the US there is a requirement that anyone coaching an affiliated soccer team involving minors must undergo an enhanced CRB check with the Criminal Record Bureau.

Managing your squad

As a coach, your job will be to teach all of the game's basic skills and, with older players, establish organization in their team play. Having a clear vision about what you want from your squad and the sort of

achievements you expect (which should be grounded in reality but challenging nonetheless), will lead you to shaping your squad for a purpose and, in turn, largely determine the content and way you organize your training sessions. It is also fair to ask yourself what your players expect from you.

A word about player discipline: it is vital to set the standards from the first session, with clear instructions about the times sessions start, expected dress code and the required standards of behavior all players should demonstrate toward coaching staff and their team-mates. Penalties (five push-ups, for example) and modest fines can be introduced with a degree of informality and humor. One of your key aims will be to create a good team spirit and it is often possible to use good-natured peer pressure to bring players into line.

Assessing your players

Not all players are made equal, and while a coach is always delighted to come across a talented player, how do you judge who is or isn't talented? You can assess the qualities and merits of young players using the following basic criteria:
• natural ability and technical skill
• awareness
• courage
• ability and speed
• enthusiasm
• anticipation
The greatest of these is anticipation. Really good players have a knack of sensing what is going to happen and consequently getting into the right position at the right time; rarely can this be coached.

For all players you should be studying their temperament: they should not get overexcited when they win or, conversely, too despondent when they lose but remain enthusiastic for the team and the game.

Assess the players by their physical attributes—size, athleticism, speed; see what ball skills they possess and determine who can dribble, receive a ball and turn and so on. I find this is best done by making the first session a series of small-sided games—usually five- or six-a-side in coned-off areas.

What you are trying to do is assess the overall ability of your squad and decide what you can realistically achieve with them.

At the start most squads will be unbalanced with far more players wanting to play in attacking positions than as defenders. You will also need to balance your team across the pitch with right- and left-footed players. This will require management by cajoling to get the right ratios.

The 90-minute training session

Every training session should follow a standard format that the players become familiar with and allows you to introduce topics and themes that will improve the team's performance over the course of the season.

The warm-up (20 minutes)
Technique and positional play drills and practices (20 minutes)
Main theme for the session (30 minutes)
An inter-squad match or one or more small-sided games (20 minutes) designed to emphasize and rehearse in a game format the coaching points made during the session.
All times are approximate. Remember to allow time for your players to cool down after the training session (see page 15).

Your theme for the session will have been determined by observing the team in action and, in all likelihood, be linked to the problem-solving (pages 127–133), or you can plan each session on a purely rotational basis. Either way you will have prepared several drills and made sure you have all the necessary equipment ready.

This book is set out in the same logical sequence that you would apply to your training session, beginning with the warm-up, then describing in detail drills for ball skills and team play; how to organize set plays; typical team performance problems and, finally, a series of small-sided, conditioned games. So, once you have determined your "theme" for the evening, you will be able to find the relevant drills, setups and small-sided games by turning to the appropriate sections.

WARM UP & COOL DOWN

The coach's role also extends to looking after the physical well-being of his players, and they should never be allowed to go into a match or a practice session where they will be expected to perform the degree of movement that soccer requires without first warming up sufficiently.

Warming up is taken very seriously throughout the professional game Even at junior level, with players as young as seven years old, there is no reason why they should not go through a short and thorough warm-up. You can use many of the warm-up routines described here, but limit them to 10–15 minutes, mixing just a few of the less strenuous exercises with jogging. Very young players need no more than 10 minutes.

You should use a designated area for warming up— do not use the field itself because there is a danger that your players will cut up the playing surface, making the skills and technical work more difficult later on. I usually work my players in pairs up and down the side of a field.

I have about 20 warm-up routines that I use in no particular order, but always start by getting the players to jog and skip up and down the length of the field. Then I mix it up, keeping the players on their toes and making sure their concentration levels stay high. After a few minutes I reduce their speed to walking pace and get them to perform five walking stretches.

Next I get them jogging again and continue with another round of five exercises, upping the tempo to raise their heart rates and finish with a further five rather more dynamic stretches. The whole warm-up for senior players should last between 15 and 20 minutes.

During this type of warm-up you do not need equipment or balls but there is nothing to stop you improvising by introducing balls as long as the players' movements are not too dynamic.

Stretching is a very technical area about which there is continued debate among the specialists in the field. The topic is too wide in scope to cover in this book, and I urge you to research stretching in detail before introducing too many dynamic stretches into your warm-up routines.

1 JOGGING
Start with a fairly slow and steady pace that can be speeded up as the intensity of the warm-up increases.

2 SKIPPING
Make sure there is plenty of bounce in the movement and the knees are kept in front of the body.

3 SIDEWAYS SHUFFLE
Keep the players moving in the same direction, but now turn them through 90°, making sure they all turn the same way! At half-distance swap over to lead with the other foot.

4 JOGGING BACKWARD
Make sure your players look over both shoulders and only have them perform the exercise for 16–22 yards (10–15m) and this must be done by all players in unison.

5 JUMP, TOUCHING SHOULDERS
As the player pairs jog forward, and after the coach's count of "one, two, three," both players jump and try to touch shoulders at the highest point of the jump. After two or three goes, reverse the position of the players. Don't allow the players to become too aggressive and make sure the players are off the ground before they barge into each other!

6 "KARAOKE" TWISTS (Picture 2)
The jogging players move one foot behind the body, and employ swiveling hips to twist the body.

7 HEELS TO BACKSIDE
The jogging players lean forward slightly and put the backs of their hands against the tops of their backsides. They continue jogging, kicking their heels up to their hands.

8 KNEES UP IN FRONT (Picture 3)
Players jog forward with a skipping motion, bring alternate knees up to the chest, or, on the coach's command, bring both knees up to waist level.

9 JUMP TO HEAD

On the coach's command the players, using a one-footed take-off, jump to head an imaginary ball. Alternate the feet on successive jumps.

10 SIMULATED VOLLEY

On the coach's command the players bring their right foot across the body to volley an imaginary ball to their left, and vice versa. Make sure the players are not too close, otherwise they will be kicking each other!

11 OPENING AND CLOSING THE GROIN

As the players jog forward, the knee is brought up to the front of the body and over to the side. Make sure both sides are worked.

12 KICKING TO OPPOSITE ARMS (Picture 4)

During a very slow jog and on the coach's command, the player kicks high to his left hand held straight out at shoulder height. Then swap legs.

13 QUICK FEET

On the coach's command the jogging players accelerate the speed of their feet, with a shuffling-like motion.

14 TURN 360°

On the coach's instruction every jogging player turns rapidly through 360°. The coach should specify left or right and make the calls at random so the players are kept guessing.

15 JOCKEYING BACKWARD

Each player adopts a slightly crouched defensive pose with the knees bent and turned 45° toward an imaginary ball. The players now twist their hips left and right as if the imaginary player in front of them is trying to get past them. This can be done in a forward or backward motion.

16 SINGLE LEG HOPS

Players take one foot off the ground and hop forward. You can add in a hop to the side or a zig-zag motion.

17 BUNNY HOPS

Resist doing this too often and too dynamically, but throw in four or five bunny hops during the jog.

18 DROP SHOULDER RIGHT, CHECK LEFT

This movement mimics a fake move that would trick an opponent. As the players jog forward and on the coach's command, they plant their right feet firmly on the ground, and drop the right shoulder. Then check to the left, plant the left foot and step away with a body swerve. Continue jogging and repeat going the other way.

19 BACKSIDES TO THE FLOOR (Picture 5)

This is a reaction exercise which I would put in toward the end of a warm-up. On the coach's command every player has to put his backside on the grass or floor and immediately get up again. It is an exercise that simulates recovery from loss of balance or fall.

20 PRESS UP TO THE FLOOR (Picture 1)

On the coach's command the players fall forward to the floor in a push-up motion using their hands to stop them falling flat on their faces. They must quickly bring their legs up and rise to a jogging position.

The cool down

Cooling down after intensive physical activity is as important as the warm-up. It slows the players' heart rate, allows them to take in fluids, and provides an opportunity for a mental debrief. A gentle jog, often linked with putting away the equipment that has been used during the training session, and a few gentle stretches are all that are usually needed. Make sure your players cool down effectively and shower after the training session, not just for reasons of hygiene but because of the beneficial effect of warm water on muscles. To avoid your players rushing off after the training session, you might like to nominate one of the more senior players to manage the cooling down session.

2

BALL SKILLS

The very foundation of the game, its bedrock if you will, lies in the ability of players to manipulate the ball effectively and to be entirely confident when in possession of it. It may be an obvious thing to say, but a group of players without either adequate control of the ball or the vision and skill to use it, render just about every other facet of the game—formations, tactics, physical presence and so on—irrelevant.

In fact, we are not just looking for "good" technique; we are seeking mastery of the ball. We also require that our players translate their hard-won skills, practiced endlessly on the training ground, into an effective competitive armory, capable of withstanding the pressure of competitive match situations.

In this section we have chosen six basic skills and techniques that every outfield player must learn and should always be looking to improve thereafter.

KICKING

Kicking uses the most important part of the soccer player's equipment—his feet—and can be defined as the ability to place the ball where it needs to go, whether it is in the air or along the ground, over ten or fifty yards (meters). Further, the best measure of the accuracy of the kick is the ease with which the receiving player can control and deal with the pass.

DRILL 1 Driving balls low

PREPARATION Two poles placed 22 yards (20m) apart.

PLAYERS Players in pairs—up to eight groups of two.

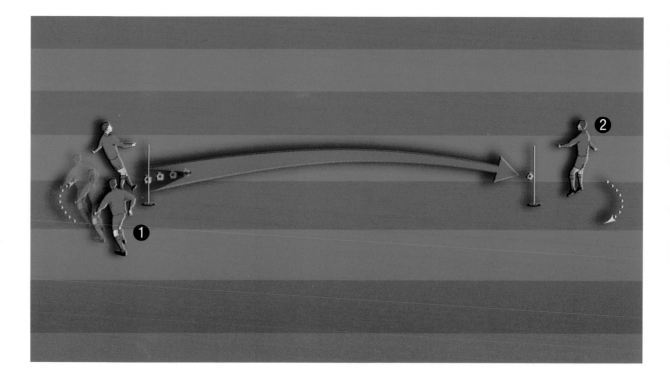

THE DRILL

• Player 1 pushes the ball to one side of the pole and drives the ball low to his partner.

• The receiving player, who is about 1 yard (1m) beyond the far side of his pole, controls the ball with his first touch, then pushes it across his body and outside the pole and finally drives it back to his partner again.

• The receiving player should try to control the ball, move it and complete his return pass using only three touches.

COACHING POINTS

This is as basic as it gets. In the first instance you should expect to see all of the players exhibit a soft touch on control and then produce a gently weighted pass to the side.

At the outset of the 22 yard (20m) pass, the player's non-kicking foot goes alongside the ball, the head stays over the ball and the eyes remain fixed firmly on it. The kick is made with a pointed toe and a firm ankle.

DRILL 2   Chipping the ball

PREPARATION One ball between two players.

PLAYERS Players in pairs—up to eight groups of two.

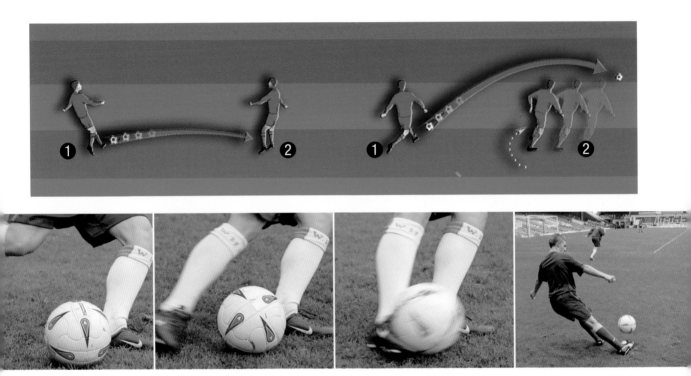

THE DRILL

• The pairs start by facing each other 6 yards (5m) apart, passing the ball back and forward in a controlled manner. After a few passes player 2 pushes the ball wide of player 1, turns and begins a run away from his partner.

• Player 1 approaches the ball and with his non-kicking foot alongside the ball, body leaning slightly backward, plants his foot underneath the ball and tries to chip it over his retreating partner. Player 2 chases down the ball, controls it and turns to face his partner again.

• Player 1 should try to chip the ball so it falls approximately 1 to 2 yards (or meters) beyond the running player. Good elevation on the chipped ball will help achieve this.

• Once player 2 has the ball under control and is facing player 1, it's player 1's turn to receive a pass, push it back wide of player 2, make his turn and run while player 2 attempts to perform the chip.

COACHING POINTS

The chipping technique consists of getting the toe underneath the ball, while the head is kept down and the body leans back. During this drill we are looking for the performing player to achieve good direction and accurate distance with his chip.

The distance the ball must be chipped into the space beyond the running player will be determined by the pace of his partner's run, and would be critical in a match situation.

DRILL 3   Kicking accurately over a longer distance

PREPARATION Two poles or cones set approximately 43 yards (40m) apart.

PLAYERS Groups of four players.

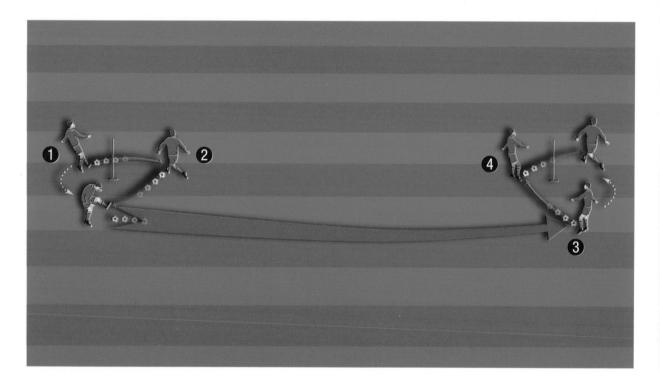

THE DRILL

• Player 1 is in possession of the ball 1 yard (1m) from the pole. Player 2 is 4 or 5 yards (or meters) behind the same pole, facing player 1.

• Player 1 passes the ball to player 2, who returns the pass but on the opposite side of the pole.

• Player 1 moves to attack and drive the ball across the 43 yards (40m) gap between the two poles and to the feet of player 3. Player 3 controls the ball and lays it back to player 4, who passes it back the other side of their pole to player 3, who now drives the ball back to player 1.

• The drill is repeated ten times and then the players swap positions.

COACHING POINTS

The greater the distance, the more likely the pass is to be inaccurate, so it is really important that you emphasize to all the players that they must really concentrate on the ball during the drill.

The pass pushed wide of the pole, which sets up the 43 yards (40m) kick, must be soft and controlled.

The kicking player must receive a pass that can be driven without the need for a controlling touch.

The kicking technique requires the player to keep his eyes on the ball, the non-kicking foot is placed alongside the ball, and with a pointed toe and a tight ankle, he kicks through the ball.

DRILL 4 Half-volley techniques

PREPARATION One ball between two players.

PLAYERS Players in pairs—up to eight groups of two.

THE DRILL

• Player 1 holds the ball in his hands and throws it head high, letting it drop and bounce.

• As the ball drops for the second time and just as the ball hits the ground he half-volleys the ball to player 2, who must control the ball by foot or by body, depending on the accuracy of the volley.

• Player 2 retrieves and picks up the ball and now repeats the drill back to his partner, player 1.

• Alternatively, the drill can be simply adapted to practice the volley, rather than the half-volley, by telling the players not to allow the ball to bounce a second time but to hit it as the ball starts to drop from the highest point of its first bounce. (Player should be discouraged from striking a rising ball, as this will often result in a lofted pass, and in so doing loss of control and accuracy.)

COACHING POINTS

A volley needs good balance and, as with all techniques related to kicking, the player must keep his eyes on the ball.

When making contact with the ball, the knee of the kicking foot should be over the ball. The kick is made with a pointed toe through the center of the ball and with a moderate follow-through.

More advanced players can flick the ball up to the half-volley or volley as shown in picture 1.

CONTROL

Control is the ability to leave the ball playable through "touch and feel." This touch has the effect of cushioning the ball—using any part of the body it comes into contact with. The player is trying to place the ball to the side and slightly in front of himself, ready for the next action.

DRILL 5   Control and pass

PREPARATION One ball and three poles set up in triangular formation 11 yards (10m) apart.

PLAYERS Groups of three players.

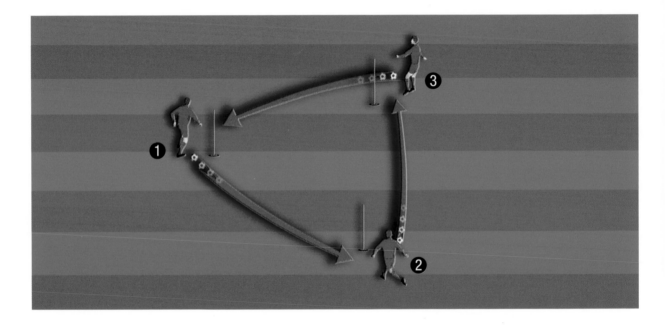

THE DRILL

• Player 1 moves the ball from the left to the right side of the pole and pushes it quite firmly to player 2. The reason for the firm pass is that we want player 2 to receive a ball that he has to actively control.

• If the drill progresses as the diagram suggests, that is from left to right (counterclockwise), player 2 will receive the ball and try to control it with the inside of his right foot, i.e. his back foot.

• As the ball makes contact with the inside of the player's foot as he adopts an open stance and relaxes the surface of his foot by pulling it away from his body, he is in effect using the foot to cushion the ball.

• At the same time he tries to push the ball slightly to the right of his pole. Then he moves the ball out of his feet and to his right to pass the ball to player 3—who repeats the drill back to player 1.

COACHING POINTS

Players should be encouraged to receive the ball on the half-turn, and with their first touch move the ball in the direction the next pass will be played— eventually progressing to using two touches only.

Reverse the direction (clockwise) to practice left-foot control.

DRILL 6   Controlling the ball with chest and thigh

PREPARATION One ball between each group of three players.

PLAYERS Groups of three players set up in a triangle formation 9 yards (8m) apart.

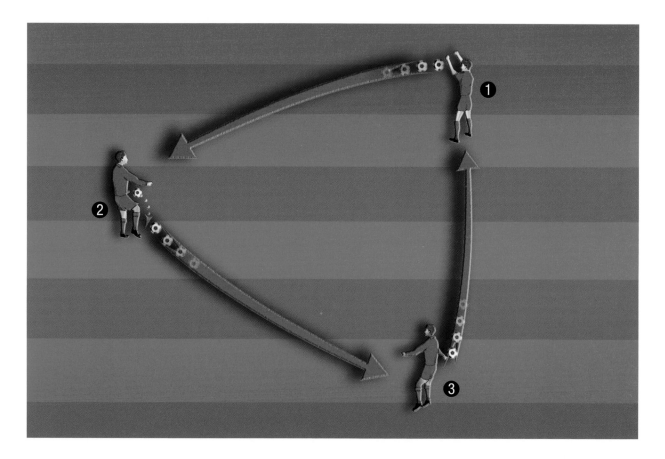

THE DRILL

• Player 1 throws the ball underarm, two-handed to player 2. As he does so he shouts out the name of the part of the body with which he wants the receiving player to control the ball—"thigh!," "chest!" and so on—and, not unreasonably, aims his throw likewise.

• Assuming it is the thigh in this case, player 2 offers his thigh to the ball and, as the ball hits that surface, withdraws it a fraction, cushioning the ball, which should now be left playable for a pass to player 3. Player 3 picks the ball up and, repeating the drill, throws underarm to player 1.

COACHING POINTS

The underarm throw ought to guarantee consistency of service to the controlling player who, in turn, must kill the ball and leave it playable. As each player attempts to control the ball, he should try to drop it to the side and in the direction of the next pass.

The finish of the sequence is a nice firm accurate pass to the receiving player.

DRILL 7   Controlling the ball on the move

PREPARATION The drill takes place in an area no larger than 22 x 22 yards (20 x 20m).

PLAYERS Groups of six players and three balls.

THE DRILL
• Three players act as servers with balls in their hands while the other three players perform the controlling technique.

• The servers remain stationary as the others jog around the area. The receivers, when they are between 9–11 yards (8–10m) away from a server with a ball, make eye contact and shout for the ball.

• The ball is served with an underarm throw to the receiver's body—at random to the thigh area, the foot or the chest. The receiving player must control the ball and return it to the server's hands; he keeps jogging around the area and receives a ball from another player.

• Swap servers and receivers after two minutes and continue the drill for at least ten minutes.

COACHING POINTS
The movement brings into play timing and the need to judge distance. The receiving player gets his body in line with the throw of the ball. Server and receiver should not get too close to each other when the ball is thrown, otherwise it will look messy and the ball will be uncontrollable; 9–11 yards (8–10m) is the minimum distance needed from the server to the receiver.

The drill can be progressed by asking the players to run randomly to any server.

DRILL 8 Controlling the ball under pressure

PREPARATION The drill takes place in a triangle between 11–22 yards (10–20m) apart

PLAYERS Three players, plus a mannequin (preferably) or pole.

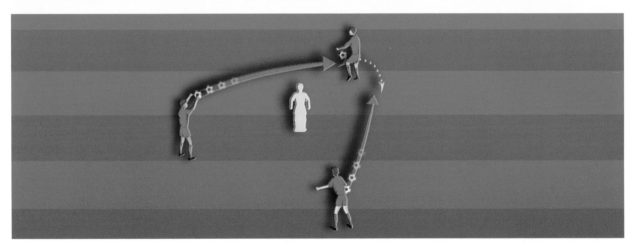

THE DRILL

• To start, the players at the base of the triangle both hold balls in their hands and remain still. The third player, at the apex of the triangle, is behind the mannequin and about 11–13 yards (10–12m) away from the players with the ball. The mannequin is positioned about two-thirds of the way between the players with the ball and the receiving player.

• The receiving player moves left or right in the direction of the next server (so there is no mannequin in the way of the oncoming ball); the server throws the ball, shouting, "thigh," "head," "chest," "foot" and so on.

• The receiving player must control the ball on the surface dictated by the server, pass the ball back to the server and move to the other side of the mannequin to receive the next ball from the second server.

• The drill is repeated 20 times, then the players rotate around the mannequin in a clockwise direction.

COACHING POINTS

The pressure on the receiving player comes from not knowing what sort of ball will come his way. For more proficient players the balls can be served at a quicker rate. Slow the rate if the player is having a problem controlling the ball.

In this drill the mannequin mimics an opponent and the receiving player must move his position to avoid it as he would in a match situation.

PASSING

Passing is what the game is all about: the ability to move the ball from one player to another, at various distances, without it being intercepted by an opponent. If your players can't pass the ball, they can't play the game—it's that simple! Passing must be constantly practiced.

DRILL 9   Passing with the side of the foot

PLAYERS A minimum of four players (although this drill will accommodate up to eight players) and one ball.

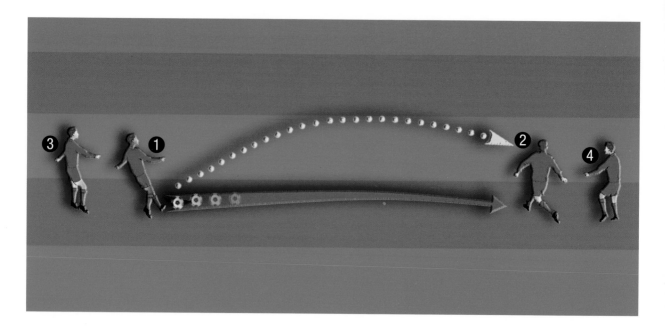

THE DRILL

• Position the players in a simple relay formation—two (or four) players at each end, 16 yards (15m) apart. Player 1 starts the drill by passing the ball along the floor to player 2, who controls the ball and passes it back to player 3.

• As player 1 completes his pass, he follows his ball and joins the group behind player 4 (or the last player at that end of the line).

• The process is repeated so that the players and the ball are in continuous motion.

COACHING POINTS

The pace of passes must not be so hard that they are wayward, uncontrollable or unplayable at the receiving end, nor so soft that the passing player arrives at the far end before his ball does!

The drill can be performed with either one (preferably) or two touches. Ideally, for advanced players, one touch to control and pass the ball will suffice, but even a novice soccer player should, after a little practice, be able to execute the drill with just two touches.

The coach should encourage the drill to flow with the minimum of interruptions or mistakes.

It can be adapted so that players pass forward and then run back to their own line.

DRILL 10 Passing in a sequence

PREPARATION Mark up an area 22 x 22 yards (20 x 20m) with a grid as shown in the diagram. If you are using six players increase the area to 22 x 33 yards (20 x 30m).

PLAYERS Four or six players (the diagram shows four players).

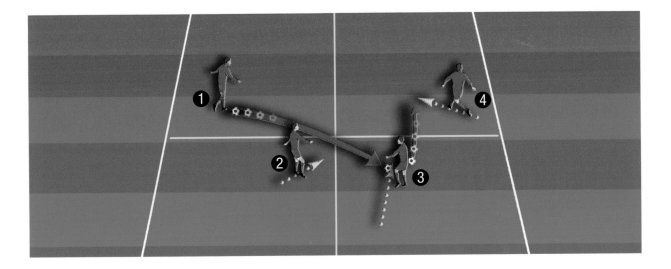

THE DRILL

• Before the drill starts, the coach gives each player a number from one to four (or six).

• In the diagram player 1 has the ball, player 2 makes himself available to receive a pass from player 1 by taking a position where player 1 can see him and is at a distance of between 5 and 17 yards (5 and 16m) away, certainly no closer than 5 yards (5m).

• Player 1 plays the ball to player 2. As player 2 is about to receive the ball, player 3 should be on the move, taking up a position visible to player 2, who now passes to him. Player 3 now looks for player 4, and so on. The sequence is repeated when player 4, or player 6, when six players are performing the drill, receives the ball and passes it back to player 1.

• The drill should last for three or four minutes, then let the players catch their breath. Ideally the whole drill should last fifteen or twenty minutes.

• The coach should make it clear from the outset how many touches each player is allowed before releasing the ball—from three to one.

COACHING POINTS

This is a good test of the technical quality of your squad's passing: is it accurate and well paced?

It also highlights the ability of receiving players to time their runs and calls for the ball. In a game situation a player must not show his hand too early, otherwise he will be marked off the ball; too close to the passing player and little territorial advantage would be gained.

During this drill, experienced players will time their runs so that they are in position to receive the ball just at the point when the passing player has, in turn, just received the ball.

The drill should flow without players holding on to the ball—control, pass, move.

DRILL 11 3 vs. 1 (keeping possession)

PREPARATION Mark up an area 16 x 11 yards (15 x 10m).

PLAYERS Three players with the ball and one defensive player to upset the rhythm.

THE DRILL

• The "attacking" players pass the ball to each other in similar fashion to the previous drill, but now we add in the pressure of a defender trying to disrupt the rhythm of their passing.

• The "defending" player needs to make realistic challenges, either intercepting the ball as it is passed or tackling the player with the ball.

• With a defender snapping at the passing player's heels, disguising the nature of the intended pass and the eventual accuracy and weight of the pass becomes more and more important.

• When an "attacking" player loses possession of the ball, he becomes the defending player, who as the sole "defender" will have to chase the ball (hard work!)—so there is an incentive to become a more skillful passer of the ball. The "attackers" should try to build up a sequence of passes, but not in numerical sequence this time.

• If the defending player fails to win the ball, there must be a time limit (usually two minutes is sufficient), otherwise he will just run himself into the ground and soon lose enthusiasm for the drill.

COACHING POINTS

Players in the early stages of their development may need several touches to control and pass the ball successfully, so give them the freedom to feel comfortable on the ball. More experienced players should be limited to one or two touches and the area can be reduced to 11 x 11 yards (10 x 10m).

While the "attackers" are trying to build up their sequence of passes, it is the defending player who largely determines how and to where the ball is passed.

Awareness of other players' movement, quick feet, quick decision making and accuracy of passing are the keys to success.

DRILL 12 Passing to a target to "score"

PREPARATION Mark out an area of 16 x 44 yards (15 x 40m).

PLAYERS Groups of eight players. There will be one target player at each end line of the area and three groups of two players identified by bibs: two red, two yellow and two white.

THE DRILL

• Before the drill starts the coach designates two defending players—in the diagram we've shown them as red-bibbed players. The coach also determines which target end the two red-bibbed players are defending (in the diagram they are defending the area to the right).

• The four attacking players (two in yellow and two in white bibs) attempt to pass the ball through and around the two defenders into the target player at the right-hand end of the area. Each time the attackers get the ball into the target player they "score" a goal.

• The ball is then returned to the four attackers who begin a fresh set of passes aiming to "score" at the opposite end this time.

• Set a time limit of two minutes and count the goals the attacking players have "scored." (The defenders might have a target of say four "goals" against them. The fewer the better.)

• Now swap the players over so that the two yellow-bibbed players become the defenders and start the stopwatch again. Keep a record of how many "goals"

each pair of defenders concedes. With a ratio of four attackers to two defenders, there should be a fairly high rate of successful passing play and "scoring."

COACHING POINTS

It is important that you set skill-level standards for this drill; for example, make it clear that for a goal to be given, the end-zone target player must receive and control the final ball. In other words, the final ball must be an accurate pass, not a wild shot.

This drill imposes a game form on a passing drill; although we have two defenders trying to win the ball and interrupt the attacking play, the drill's emphasis is on passing skills (not shooting or tackling).

The drill is designed to develop movement and improve player awareness.

Conditions can be applied to the drill: all passes must be below head height so that the attackers have to play around and through defenders rather than over them and, if the players are of a good standard, limit the amount of touches each attacking player is allowed.

BALL MASTERY

At the beginning of this section I said that we needed our players to have mastery over the ball, and here I have identified six basic ball mastery skills that every player must add to their repertoire of skills. They are, in many ways, both the heart and foundations of the game —the building blocks to success—requiring touch, practice, soccer-intelligence and confidence. I've prepared three drills for each of the six skills in increasing levels of difficulty.

DRILL 13 Keep the ball up—one touch and bounce

PREPARATION A ball for each player.

THE DRILL
• This is about improving your players' touch and developing their feel for the ball. You should see every player improve his ability to sustain this drill over the course of the season.

• Each player starts with the ball in his hands and throws it into the air about head height before letting it bounce. As it does so he tries to kick the ball in the air again to just below head height, lets it bounce again, and repeats the kick.

• Players should use either foot—at this stage we simply want them to develop a touch and a feel for the ball.

• The ball should go straight up in line with the player's body (not to the side), and climb no higher than the head.

COACHING POINT
The whole squad can take part in this drill at the same time, and the coach should offer encouragement and advice as necessary. Don't be afraid to stop the session if you identify a common mistake.

DRILL 14 One bounce and continuous with one foot

PREPARATION A ball for each player.

THE DRILL
• As in the previous drill, each player starts with the ball in his hands, throws the ball into the air about head height and lets it bounce.

• This time before the ball drops to the ground for the second time, the player tries to get several touches on the ball using one foot.

• Once the player loses control of the ball, he picks it up and repeats the exercise using his other foot.

DRILL 15 Keep up continuously with both feet

PREPARATION A ball for each player.

THE DRILL
• Repeat the start of the drill, but this time the players must keep the ball up continuously using the right and left foot alternatively.

• We are looking for the player to get as many continuous touches of the ball as possible and if, from time to time, the player has to "catch" the ball by using the same foot, don't stop the drill—as long as the weaker foot is being used throughout the drill.

COACHING POINTS
The player should be relaxed and impart just enough energy so the ball reaches chest height. The arms and shoulders should be relaxed and out to the side to aid balance.

A good coach should never forget that the game itself is simple. Good coaching is all about breaking down the game's technical requirements into an understandable form and developing drills to refine these basic skills.

Step-over and move

Using body movement and weight transfer to trick an opponent are the hallmarks of many great players and something we want to teach players from an early age. Actually, most youngsters revel in the chance to practice tricks and fakes, so this is usually a popular training session! However, for young players to master this skill they must start at the most basic level and really get to grips with the mechanics of the technique—in slow motion if necessary. The game needs skillful dribblers, so spend plenty of time on the next three drills.

DRILL 16 A simple step-over

PREPARATION A ball for each player.

THE DRILL
• The ball is placed on the ground in front of the player, who begins the drill bouncing on his toes: you don't want the players standing around flat-footed at the outset of the drill.

• The player throws the outside of his right foot over the ball and plants it firmly just beyond the ball. All his weight is now on his right foot and right side.

• The shift in body weight means that his left foot is released, allowing the outside of the left foot to be used to push the ball to the left and into space.

• At this point we do not require the players to move with the ball, we just want them to feel and understand the mechanics of what the feet are doing.

• The player retrieves his ball and repeats the drill several times. Now swap feet and repeat several more times.

COACHING POINT
This is a very static exercise designed to help players sort their feet out. It must be practiced on both sides, remembering that one side is always going to be favored, and even a simple drill like this will feel a little awkward on the weaker foot.

DRILL 17 Step-over and push away

PREPARATION A ball for each player.

THE DRILL

• Now we are going to add movement to the step-over, pushing the ball away and making the drill altogether more lifelike.

• From the starting position, the player simulates running forward with the ball—slowly pushing the ball along the ground. On either the coach's command or, in free practice, when the player feels comfortable, he steps over the ball with his left foot and pushes the ball 2 yards (2m) to his right with his right foot, or 2 yards (2m) to his left with his left foot when he steps over with his right foot.

• To repeat: when the drill is first introduced, it is carried out at a gentle walking pace. The tempo can be upped as players get used to the mechanics of the drill.

DRILL 18 Trick your opponent

PREPARATION Pairs of players both with a ball facing each other 11 yards (10m) apart.

THE DRILL

• The players run toward each other at a gentle pace and on one player's signal, "yes," "now" or "let's go," both perform the same drill: step-over with the right foot and push away with the left foot—if they mistakenly perform "opposite" step-overs they'll end up running into each other.

• Once both players have completed the right foot step-over, they turn round, and, making sure they are 11 yards (10m) apart, repeat the drill. As proficiency grows, the better players will begin to add speed.

• At this point we can introduce the double step-over: the technique is much the same—the player steps over with his left foot, but instead of pushing away with the right foot he then steps over with his right foot, comes back and pushes away with his left foot.

Turns

Players who can turn quickly with the ball and change the direction of the play or attack the opposition very quickly are in possession of a skill that should never be underestimated.

DRILL 19 Back-foot turn

PREPARATION A mannequin, mimicking a defender, is useful but not absolutely essential.

PLAYERS Groups of three.

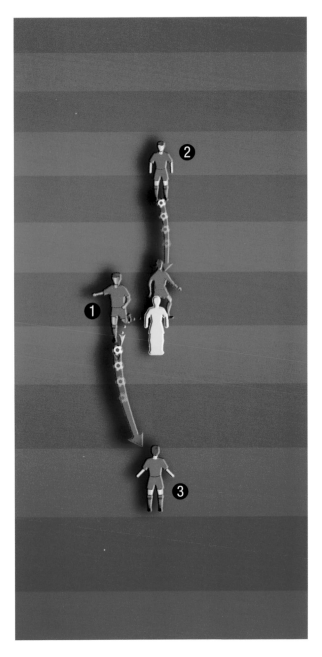

THE DRILL

• This drill simulates an attacker "coming off" a defender, turning him and making a pass into the space behind the defender or running at him.

• Player 2, who starts the drill, and player 3 are spaced 22 yards (20m) apart. Player 1 stands in front, and slightly to the side, of the mannequin on the half-turn. Looking at the diagram you can see that player 1's shoulders are at an angle of 45° to player 2, in what is called an open position on the half-turn.

• Player 2 passes the ball along the ground to player 1. Player 1 controls the ball with his back foot—i.e. the foot that is farthest from the ball as it is passed (in this case the right foot).

• Now he pulls the ball behind him with his first touch, and then turns on his front foot to face player 3. Finally, player 1 passes the ball out of his feet to player 3. Player 3 repeats the drill in the opposite direction.

• The player in position 1 performs the drill eight or ten times and then swaps position with either 2 or 3. Make sure everyone has a turn.

COACHING POINT

Generally, you will find that players tend to favor one foot over the other, but in the early stages of a player's development, the coach should encourage the use of both feet; if anything, emphasize the weaker side.

DRILL 20 Back-foot turn with added movement

PREPARATION A mannequin, mimicking a defender, is useful but not absolutely essential.

PLAYERS Groups of three.

THE DRILL

• The set-up is the same as the previous drill, but now we add movement by the receiving player away from the "defending" mannequin and toward the passing player.

• The receiving player, player 1, is now required to dictate when he wants the ball passed.

• His starting position must be within touching distance of the mannequin and, as he calls for the ball, he steps away at an angle creating approximately 2 yards (2m) of space between himself and the mannequin before the ball arrives at his back foot.

• The turn is executed as in the previous drill, with the added pressure of completing the technique while moving toward the ball. The ball is passed through to player 3 and the drill is repeated in the opposite direction.

• The drill is a good simulation of creating the space to "come off" a defender and turning him—a vital skill for any attack-minded player during a game.

DRILL 21 Back-foot turn—groups of four

PREPARATION A mannequin, mimicking a defender, and six poles placed 2 yards (2m) apart, three at each end.

PLAYERS Groups of four.

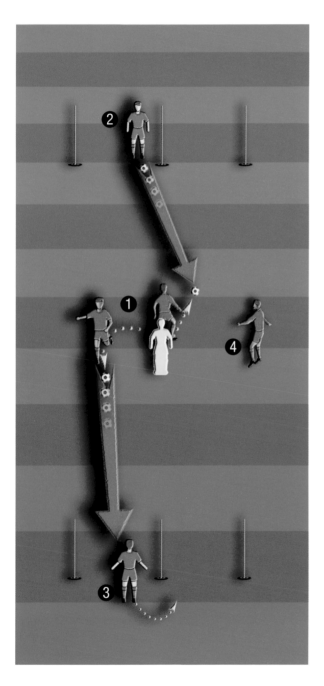

THE DRILL

• The added difficulty during this drill is that the direction of the final pass to player 3 by the performing player is now dictated by the variable position of player 3, who is no longer a static target.

• The drill follows the sequence of movement and passing as previously described, however player 3 can now opt to position himself in either of the "gates" created between the poles.

• Therefore player 1, as he makes his turn, has to pick out his teammate, and make an accurate pass to complete the drill.

• Once player 3 has the ball, he passes it from his right-hand gate to player 4, who has taken up a position on the opposite side of the mannequin to player 1. He now repeats the drill, turning and finding player 2 with his pass.

Fake moves and change of pace

I make no apology for including a second set of drills designed to improve the ability of young players to trick their opponents, because players who can create a little bit of space and take opposing players out of the game—and in the process often bring about an advantageous 2 versus 1 situation somewhere on the pitch—are hugely valuable to both their team and the game in general.

DRILL 22 Dropping the shoulder

PREPARATION You will need a mannequin.

PLAYERS Groups of three players, two placed either side of a mannequin, facing each other separated by approximately 22 yards (20m) and a third player approximately 6 yards (5m) in front of the mannequin.

THE DRILL

• The performing player, who is 6 yards (5m) in front of the mannequin, uses the inside of his right foot to take the ball slowly up to the left of the mannequin and, at a point about a yard (meter) from it, drops his left shoulder and pushing off from his left foot manipulates the ball with the outside of his right foot, pushing the ball to the right side of the mannequin.

• Once past the mannequin he passes the ball to the waiting player, who repeats the drill.

COACHING POINTS

It is important that at the point the player makes his "move," it is performed with speed and precision.

Drills that simulate fake moves and turns need to be practiced often and repeatedly before the techniques and skills become habit and are used instinctively and effectively in matches.

DRILL 23 Everybody on the move

PREPARATION Mark out an area 22 x 22 yards (20 x 20m). Note: you don't necessarily have to mark it up with grids as shown in the diagram.

PLAYERS Groups of six players with three balls.

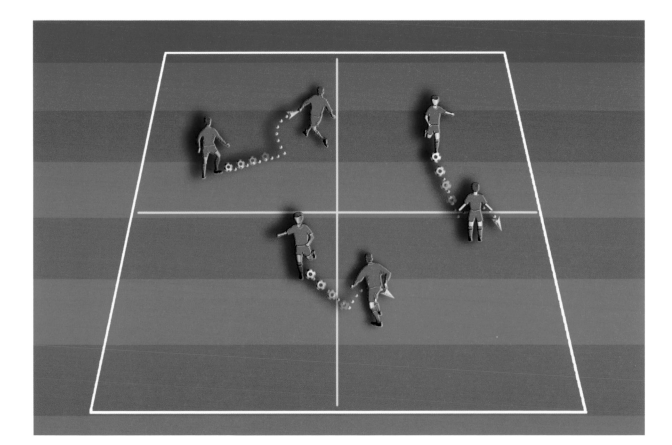

THE DRILL

• Now we put two of our groups of three players together to form a practicing unit of six—three with a ball each and three without.

• The three players without a ball are the equivalent of moving mannequins and are not trying to actively win possession of the ball, but behave as objects for the performing players to work around and practice against. This will help prevent them working in a straight line.

• The drill starts with everyone on the move. The players in possession of the balls run about the marked area with the ball at their feet. They must avoid running into space occupied by another dribbling player and constantly perform a fake move and change of pace as they randomly encounter the "defenders."

• To gain full benefit from this drill, run it for one and a half minutes, then swap the roles. The drill should be performed continuously for fifteen minutes without interruption, changing roles constantly.

DRILL 24 1 vs. 1 competitive situation

PREPARATION Mark out an area 32 x 11 yards (30 x 10m) and create a "goal" at each end with poles or cones set 2 yards (2m) apart.

PLAYERS Two players with a ball.

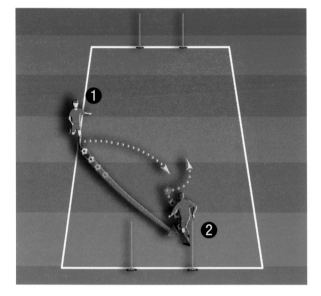

THE DRILL

• Superficially, this is a remarkably simple drill, but it replicates a game-like situation and requires the performing player to use his fake move and change of pace skills intelligently and competitively.

• The drill starts as player 1, who is positioned 16–22 yards (15–20m) up and to the side of the "field," passes the ball to the feet of player 2, who is in the end area in front of the goal. Player 2 has to "score" at the far end.

• Player 1 immediately follows his pass on to the "field" and does his best to close down and tackle player 2 to win the ball.

• Player 2 uses fake moves and changes of pace to beat player 1. Unlike in the previous drills, which practiced these skills in a methodical and unopposed way, the performing player now has to decide when and how he will employ the skills while under pressure. It will not only test the player's ability to perform the skills, but also his decision-making and timing.

• Once player 2 has scored or the defender has gained possession of the ball, roles are swapped and the drill is repeated. As an alternative, we can make the goals larger and add goalkeepers.

COACHING POINTS

If your players are not quite ready for this more advanced drill, you can ask the defending player to remain passive and not compete for the ball too aggressively.

We are trying to encourage the performing player to have confidence, and be positive about, using his fake move and change of direction skills when up against opposition. Say to your players, "Don't be afraid to try."

Receive and change direction

You regularly see players play the ball back to the part of the field where the ball has just come from, which is usually the most crowded area. If a player can receive the ball in one area and change direction of the play by playing it into another, then his team can move the opposition around quickly and take advantage of free space.

DRILL 25 Groups of three

PREPARATION Set up a triangle of poles as shown in the diagram. Each player stands approximately 1 yard (meter) in front of a pole.

PLAYERS Groups of three players organized in a triangular formation.

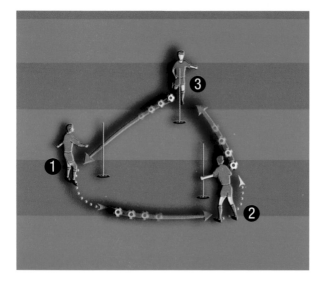

THE DRILL

• Player 1 passes the ball to player 2, who is on the half-turn facing player 1.

• When he receives the ball he lets the ball run across his body on to his back foot—in this case his right foot—and controls it and maneuvers the ball beyond the right side of the pole, finally pushing the ball to player 3, who has moved to his left and is facing player 2 on the half-turn.

• Players of all abilities should try to perform the drill using only two touches of the ball.

• After several circuits, reverse the direction so that the players practice with both feet.

DRILL 26 Groups of four

PREPARATION Mark out an area 11 x 11 yards (10 x 10m).

PLAYERS Groups of four players.

THE DRILL

• In this drill we set up a 3 vs. 1 situation. The player shown in the diagram wearing red is trying to win the ball from the other three players.

• Player 1 is passing to player 2 on his right, away from the defending player, who is trying to gain possession. Player 2 opens his body out to receive the ball with his right foot and can pass with either one or two touches to player 3, who is waiting on his right.

• This is a constantly moving picture and not every pass or technique will be completed successfully, nor will every pass result in a change of direction because of the efforts of the red defender. He may cut off the would-be-passer's angle, forcing him to play it back to the player from whom he received the ball, but at every opportunity we want the

players to receive the ball from one direction, control it and move it in another.

COACHING POINTS

The player that is caught in possession or loses possession or passes it out of play becomes the defender, and roles are swapped over very quickly. Players are rewarded for keeping the ball and punished—they will end up being the defender for most of the time—if they constantly give the ball away!

If your players are not yet at a level to handle this drill, make the defender a little more static or passive; he should still be moving, but not challenging hard for the ball. The other options are to add an extra attacker or make the area larger.

DRILL 27 Groups of six

PREPARATION Mark out an area 22 x 22 yards (20 x 20m).

PLAYERS Groups of six players.

THE DRILL

• This is an enhancement of the previous drill in which we have two bibbed players acting as defenders trying to win the ball and four players whose job it is to keep possession, manipulate the ball and change the direction of play—playing the ball between and around the back of the two defenders.

• Again, if you find that this drill is too difficult, you can do one of three things: ask the defenders to act more passively, add another attacker or make the area a bit bigger so that the defenders have more space to cover.

The half-volley sweep

With this next set of drills I have tried to develop one simple skill to deal with a ball that is dropping out of the air. I have already mentioned control and touch earlier, so now I want to concentrate on the sweep. It is exactly what it says it is. At its simplest as the ball drops out of the air and hits the ground, the player sweeps it away on the half-volley.

DRILL 28 Simple half-volley sweep 1

PREPARATION A ball for each player.

THE DRILL

• The player throws the ball into the air about twice his body height, and as it begins its descent moves his body into line with the ball, keeping his eyes firmly fixed on it.

• Just as the ball hits the ground, and at the beginning of its bounce, he sweeps it away to the left with the inside of his right foot.

• Technically speaking, as the ball drops the player's weight is on his left foot. The right foot comes off the ground to anticipate the bounce and, as it bounces, the ball is swept with the inside of the right foot across the body to the left.

COACHING POINT

This drill, and the skill itself in match situations, requires a good touch and feel for the ball, because it is easy for the player to over-hit the ball, sending it 22 yards (20m) or more away. In a match situation this would almost certainly mean losing possession. Ideally, the ball should travel 6 yards (5m) or so.

DRILL 29 Simple half-volley sweep 2

PREPARATION You will need a mannequin positioned between each pair of players.

PLAYERS Groups of two players with a ball between them.

THE DRILL

• Once the actual technique of half-volleying the ball away is mastered, we increase the difficulty of the drill and make things more realistic by varying the height and direction of the ball, now thrown by a second player, and by restricting the receiving player's view of the ball by interposing a mannequin between him and his partner.

• This very simple drill consists of player 1 throwing the ball over the mannequin to his partner, who is 2 or 3 yards (2 or 3m) beyond the mannequin. Player 2 sweeps the ball away on the half-volley with the inside or the outside of his foot.

DRILL 30 Simple half-volley sweep 3

PREPARATION Mark out an area of 11 x 11 yards (10 x 10m) for each two-player group.

PLAYERS Groups of two players with a ball each.

THE DRILL

• The players stand facing each other approximately 9 yards (8m) apart. Both have a ball in their hands and on a signal (either a count to three or the coach's whistle) they throw their balls in the air to each other, slightly to one side and twice the height of their partner.

• As it descends both players sweep what was his partner's ball away on the half-volley.

• The players retrieve the ball they have volleyed and repeat the exercise.

COACHING POINTS

You are looking for a controlled half-volley sweep. The players should meet the ball just as it bounces, sweeping the ball away to the right with the inside of the left foot and vice versa.

In order to replicate a match situation when maintaining team possession of the ball is vital. During this drill players must keep close control of the ball; it is important that the touch they impart is sufficient for the ball to travel no more than 6 yards (5m) and to stay in the 11 yards (10m) area.

HEADING

Being able to head the ball well is a vital skill for every player, no matter what their position—and that includes goalkeepers! It can create and score goals or intercept and deal with dangerous attacking situations. For young players, heading the ball should be introduced slowly and sympathetically. As they progress more demands can be made, but try not to put them off by expecting too much too soon.

DRILL 31 Heading technique to build confidence

PREPARATION The players stand facing each other 11 yards (10m) apart. A ball for each pair.

PLAYERS Groups of two players.

THE DRILL

• Player 1 throws the ball two-handed underarm to the head of player 2, who heads the ball back to player 1.

• Since the drill is designed to develop the players' heading technique, the coach can insist that the receiving player heads the ball twice. He first heads the ball vertically and then, after it drops, heads it back to player 1.

• Player 2 should perform ten headers and then alternate with his partner. At this stage you are not asking the players to jump for the ball.

COACHING POINTS

This simple drill is designed to instill confidence into your players and help develop good technique as they learn to head the ball.

Players must watch the ball right on to their foreheads, use their arms in an open position for balance, thrust the neck toward the ball, arch the back and keep their eyes open for as long as possible (there will be a blinking motion when the ball makes contact). Young players commonly make the mistake of closing their eyes well before the ball arrives.

DRILL 32 Heading the ball on the move

PREPARATION Two balls (initially use just one ball, but as the players become familiar with the drill, introduce a second ball).

PLAYERS Groups of six players.

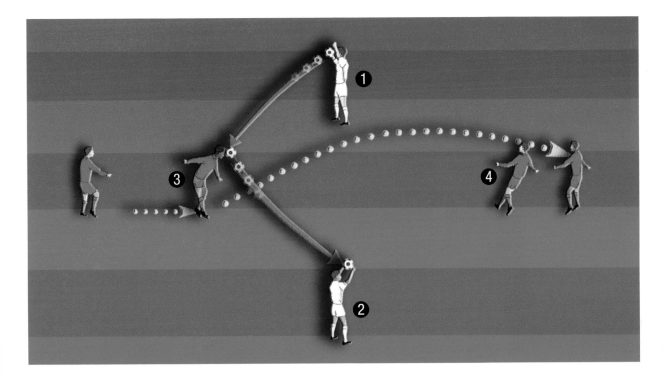

THE DRILL

• Six players are placed in a diamond formation.

• Players 1 and 2, who are approximately 11 yards (10m) apart, act as servers. The remaining players, split evenly, wait at the side of the diamond.

• The drill commences as player 1 throws the ball two-handed underarm to player 3, who is running from the right side of player 1. Player 3 heads the ball in the direction of player 2.

• Player 2 catches the ball and throws it to his right to player 4, who is making his run. Player 4 heads the ball back to player 1.

• After heading the ball, the performing players continue their runs and rejoin the line of waiting players on the opposite side of the diamond.

• Once the players' confidence and skill level are sufficient and the players understand the sequence, a second ball can be introduced. Now the drill is all about timing of the runs as well as accuracy of heading, as players make their runs on both the left and right hand sides simultaneously.

• After a few serves players 1 and 2 alternate with two other players, and the drill continues. From time to time the players must change direction so that they receive and head from both sides.

DRILL 33 Heading in the air

PREPARATION The players stand facing each other, 11–16 yards (10–15m) apart. A ball for each pair.

PLAYERS Groups of two players.

THE DRILL

• To introduce a note of realism into the drill, ask the serving player to drop the ball on to his foot and volley it in the air to the receiving player. We are not looking for great height or distance on the ball, but for a realistic delivery replicating how a ball would be received during a game.

• If the accuracy of the volleying is wayward and the receiving player is not getting a consistent service, then revert to a throw. Of course, by introducing the volley the players are practicing an additional skill.

• The heading player must not be standing still when he receives the ball. He should be 10–12 yards (10–12m) away as the ball is served and position himself 1 yard (1m) or so in front of where he expects to meet the ball in order that he can take a couple of strides into the ball, employing a one-footed take-off and meeting the ball in the air.

• His arms should be out to the side providing balance, back arched and his head thrown toward the ball with eyes open. The ball is headed back firmly in the direction of the serving player, who will have moved 3–4 yards (3–4m) to his side after volleying or throwing the ball.

• Again, to replicate what happens during a game, the drill is designed so that the server volleys the ball to a player on the move, and by moving to the side after his volley forces the heading player to adjust his body position so that his header is directed toward the new position of the server.

• The ball should be headed to the feet of the server, who now has the additional challenge of controlling the ball. Alternatively, when practicing defensive heading we ask the player to head for height and distance.

DRILL 34 Heading for distance

PREPARATION Groups of three players with one ball. Players 1 and 2 are 33 yards (30m) apart and player 3 is 11 yards (10m) from player 1.

PLAYERS Groups of two players.

THE DRILL

• The exercise begins with player 3 playing a simple set-up pass to the side and right of player 1, who runs toward the ball and chips it in the air to player 2. Player 3 turns and runs toward heading player 2.

• Player 2 must now read the flight of the lofted ball, get in line and time his one-footed jump so that he heads the ball back over player 3, who will then turn back to player 1 and complete the drill.

• Player 2 has ten goes, then player 1 becomes 2, 2 becomes 3 and 3 becomes 1.

COACHING POINTS

This is a reasonably advanced drill and one of its key components is the quality of the chip. It will need to be accurate, supplying a consistent service for the heading player.

If this consistency is missing, you should continue working at a slightly different level by positioning the players closer together but maintaining the same technical elements and delivery of the ball by hand and volley. The two pictures above on the right show an attacking player heading the ball to the feet of an oncoming striker while being pressured by a defender.

SHOOTING

Effective shooting is all about timing and accuracy; power comes later. Good shooting technique should be honed when players are young.

A good goalscorer is an opportunist, not afraid to miss, who will keep coming back for more. It is important to encourage players to shoot at every opportunity, but not at the expense of better-placed teammates.

DRILL 35 Shooting for accuracy

PREPARATION Two poles placed at the intersection of the "D" and the penalty area. Use a full-size goal and work around the penalty area. You will need ten or more balls—four or five on the left and the same on the right.

PLAYERS The drill can accommodate a large number of players, but the ideal number is between six and eight. Any more and the waiting time between shots gets too long. You will need a goalkeeper.

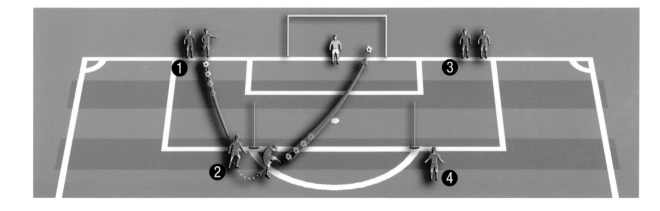

THE DRILL

• Player 1, on the left side of the goal, passes the ball to player 2, who controls the ball on the left side of the pole, moves the ball to the right side of the pole and hits his shot with the right foot on his second (or possibly third for less experienced players) touch. Ideally, it's right-foot control, right-foot shot and vice versa.

• During this drill we want to keep the ball on the limits of the penalty area and not to encroach into the penalty area to shoot.

• After the shot player 3, on the right side of the goal, passes the ball to player 4, who controls the pass and moves the ball to the left side of the pole before shooting left-footed at the goal.

• Player 1 becomes player 2 and player 2 joins the line on the left side of the goal.

COACHING POINTS

The pass into the penalty area for the shooting player must be accurate and firmly weighted (see passing skills, page 26–27).

Players on the right side of the penalty area shoot with their left foot and players on the left of the penalty area shoot right-footed.

DRILL 36 Shooting for the goal with a bouncing ball

PREPARATION The drill is carried out on half of a field, and you will need plenty of balls to maintain a good supply to the strikers.

PLAYERS The ideal number of outfield players is between six and eight, but the drill can cope with more. Two goalkeepers—there will be plenty of work to do.

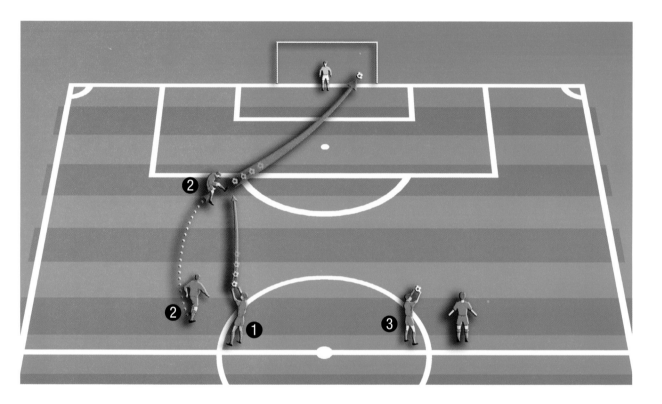

THE DRILL

• The players start just inside their own attacking half. The serving players stand either side of the center circle with a ball in their hands.

• Looking at the diagram, player 1, on the left side of the centre circle, throws the ball in throw-in fashion (not underarm this time) toward the "D" at the point it intersects with the penalty area. The ball should be bouncing as player 2 runs on to it, and he should hit it with his left foot.

• Player 2 retrieves his ball from wherever it has ended up and brings it back to the line of waiting players. Player

1 becomes player 2. Player 3 begins the sequence again on the right side. Goalkeepers can swap after ten shots—depending on the accuracy of the shooting they may get lots of action or no action at all.

COACHING POINT

Apart from practicing the timing of the run on to the bouncing ball, this drill emphasizes the importance of striking the ball as it starts to drop from the top of its bounce. Players need to learn not to strike a rising ball which will almost certainly lift over the crossbar, whereas a dropping ball is more likely to stay down.

DRILL 37 The cut-back

PREPARATION The drill is carried out on half of a field and you will need plenty of balls to maintain a good supply to the strikers. Place two poles just inside the intersection of the "D" with the penalty area.

PLAYERS The ideal number of outfield players is between six and eight, but the drill can cope with more. You can alternate between the two goalkeepers in your squad if you have them—there will be plenty of work to do.

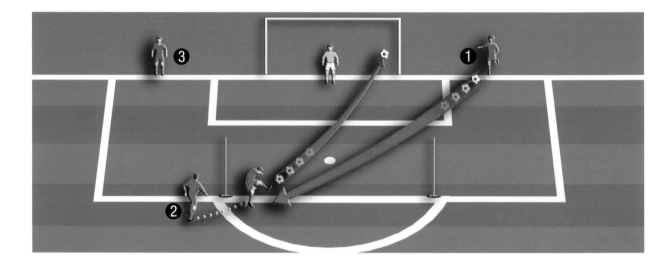

THE DRILL

• Two players assume the role of servers, on both the left and right sides of the goal, standing on the goal line between the six-yard box and the penalty area.

• Player 1, acting as server, passes the ball "back" in the direction of player 2 who, from the left of the pole, runs on to it. Player 2 should strike the ball at the goal right-footed from just inside the penalty area.

• He retrieves his ball and rejoins the group on the same side from which he started. Player 3 now passes in for the waiting player on the other side. Players starting on the left of the goal will shoot right-footed and those starting on the right will shoot left-footed.

• The coach asks the players to swap over after a dozen shots each so players work on their weaker foot.

COACHING POINTS

The ball will be rolling toward the striking player so he must not lean back, or the ball will sail up and away as he makes his shot.

During this drill the striking player can use two shooting techniques: either he guides the ball into the goal in passing fashion using the inside of the foot, or strikes the ball with more pace and power using the front of the foot with a pointed toe, leaning into it and with the knee over the ball. Remember, accuracy first before power.

The coach can insist with less practiced players that they use the passing style shot so they can concentrate on their movement toward the ball, encouraging accuracy. As the skills improve and confidence grows, then the power and pace can be added.

DRILL 38 Turn, run and shoot

PREPARATION The drill is carried out on half of a field. Two mannequins are positioned midway between the halfway line and the edge of the penalty area as shown in the diagram. You will need plenty of balls to maintain a good supply to the strikers.

PLAYERS Ten to twelve outfield players or, if you want to isolate, say, your forwards, then six to eight. One or more goalkeepers.

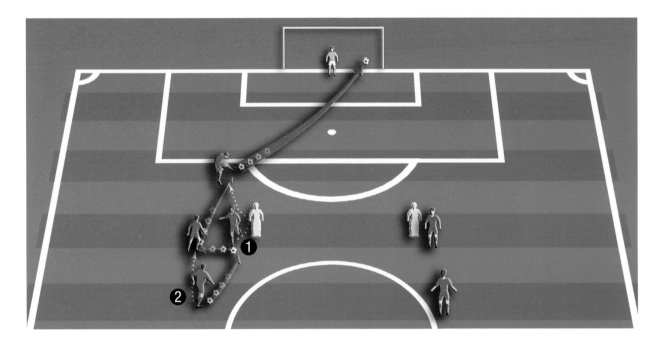

THE DRILL

• Player 1 on the left side of the diagram will receive a ball from player 2.

• Player 2 begins the drill by playing an underhit pass to player 1, who is forced to come short away from the "defending" mannequin to collect the ball and return it to the left of player 2 ("setting up play").

• Player 2, who has moved wide to receive the ball from player 1, immediately plays the ball into space to the left and behind player 1.

• Player 1 immediately spins, turns and runs on to the ball and shoots left-footed at the goal.

• Player 1 retrieves his ball and rejoins the waiting group of players on the left side of the field. Player 2 now becomes player 1 and another player from the waiting group becomes player 2.

• Alternate between the left and right side of the field.

COACHING POINT

This drill is all about the accuracy and pacing of the final pass. If player 2's pass is too heavy, the ball will run through to the goalkeeper. The coach should make it clear that player 2's responsibility is to pass the ball with just the right pace for player 1 to receive the ball on the edge of the penalty area. Learning to pass into space is not easy and takes practice.

3

TEAM PLAY

Team play is about the combining of skills and techniques to produce sound defensive habits, quick, decisive attacking play and developing habits on the training field and consistency in matches to become an effective team.

The coach must convince all of his players that they have a defensive role when the game situation demands it—even the out-and-out strikers.

The drills in this section will give your players a basic armory of defending skills and help you organize the team defensively.

Good attacking play is the product of organization and hours of practice on the training field. The coach must identify the special attacking talents of his team and play to their strengths.

Don't expect your players to always play instinctively: if, for example, players practice getting on to the end of early crosses, they are more likely to reproduce the habit during a game—which could make all the difference.

Quick, accurate passing, defense-splitting crosses and powerful shots on goal are exciting to watch, but rely on high levels of skill and technique honed on the training ground. Providing the drills and the structured practice sessions is the coach's job. And it's very satisfying when it all comes together.

DEFENDING

DRILL 39 Dealing with direct play 1

If your opponents constantly take the direct route to your goal with long high balls or try to play passes in behind your back four, then you will want to know that they are up to the job of dealing with this type of attack.

PREPARATION The drill is carried out on a full-sized field.

PLAYERS You will need sixteen players, including two goalkeepers: two sets of "back fours," two forwards in opposition to each defensive line and four ball servers, who are shown in the diagram as red and white players 1 and 2.

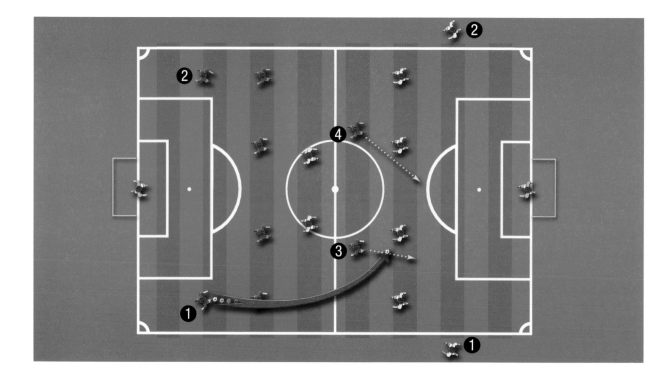

THE DRILLS

• Start the drill with either the goalkeepers or servers trying to play a long ball, preferably in the air, behind the opposing defense. In Drill 39, an attacking player red 1 plays the ball long into white's defensive line.

• Red forwards 3 and 4 try to get in behind the back line to score, but note, it's important that the attackers observe the offside law, otherwise the drill is both unrealistic and will introduce bad habits.

• White servers 1 and 2 move to the side and off the field when the red team attacks.

• An alternative version of this drill (Drill 40) involves removing the servers and using the goalkeepers to deliver the ball. You will also need to position both a red and white player centrally, as shown in the diagram to the right.

• The goalkeeper kicks long into the reds' back line. Now try to encourage continuous play by the defending side,

heading or volleying back into whites' half. The forwards try to anticipate and run in behind the white back line.

• Stop the drill when play goes dead and restart with the goalkeeper playing a long ball forward.

COACHING POINTS

The main purpose of the drill is to teach the defending team to deal with the long ball. As the ball arrives they should react by either heading or volleying it away directly before it bounces.

Defenders must be ready to deal with this type of play with the opposition always looking to turn them around and get in behind them. They must not let the ball bounce but keep together in a line, stay narrow when the ball is central and keep communicating.

They will also need to get used to pushing up as a defensive line, trapping the forwards offside. Encourage the defenders off the ball to take up covering positions automatically.

The fullbacks must not be deeper than the central defenders. If the ball drops into the midfield, then the two central red and white players keep the drill going by putting it back in behind the opposition.

Using the goalkeepers to deliver the ball will ensure that the drill can be built into continuous play.

DRILL 40 Dealing with direct play 2

Alternatively, with a squad of 14 players, the goalkeepers put the ball into play by kicking high and long, requiring the defenders to head or volley the ball back for their forwards to run on to.

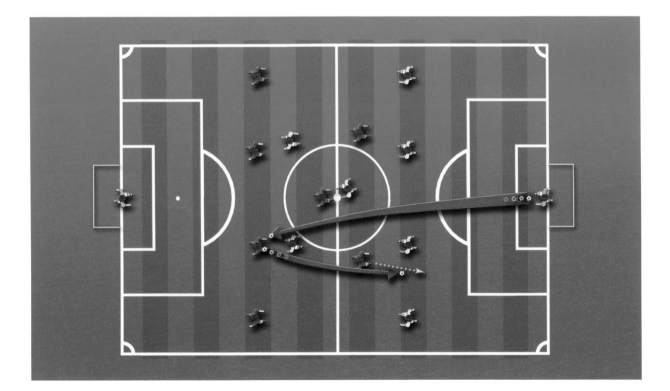

DEFENDING IN MIDFIELD

DRILL 41 Closing down the opposition

PREPARATION Start by marking out one or more areas of 11 x 33 yards (10 x 30m).

PLAYERS You will need groups of six players for each marked-out area.

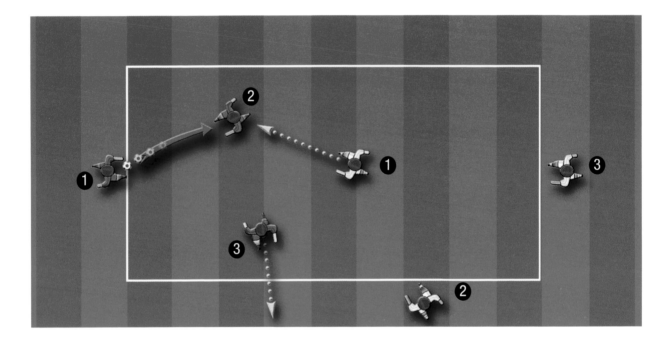

THE DRILL

• The drill starts when red server 1 passes the ball to either attacking player 2 or 3 (the player to whom the pass is not directed drops out). White player 1, acting as a defending midfielder, reacts to the pass by closing down the pass receiver and trying to stop him passing through to white server 3.

• Once the attacking player has made his pass to the opposition server, or the defending midfielder has won the ball or has run it out of play, the drill is repeated from the opposite end. Players rotate positions throughout the drill.

COACHING POINTS

Midfielders have a vital role in stopping the opposition's attacking buildup by trying to stop the ball being passed forward.

The aim of the drill is to improve the ability of midfield players to gain possession of the ball and break up the opposition's play.

You will be working on the defending midfielder's angle of approach to the pass receiver and at the same time encouraging them not to dive in and to stay on their feet. They will have to time their intervention carefully and their aim should be to block the pass, gain possession or run the ball out of bounds.

This drill can be advanced by allowing the receiving player to play a pass back to the server, who returns the ball as the receiving player attempts to lose his marker through movement. The marker must stay with the runner and not chase the ball.

DRILL 42 Going with runners

PREPARATION Start by marking out one or more areas of 16 x 33 yards (15 x 30m).

PLAYERS You will need groups of six players for each marked-out area.

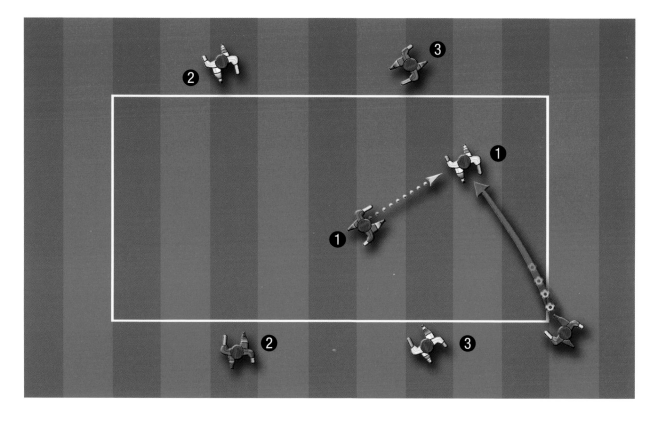

THE DRILL

• The coach acts as the server and begins the drill by passing the ball to attacking player white 1.

• Defending midfielder red 1 tries to close down the attacker, while attacker white 1 does his best to beat the approaching defender and run the ball over the end line.

• The attacking player can use players 2 and 3 positioned outside the area as teammates, playing a wall pass off them. Players 2 and 3 should be restricted to a maximum of two touches before releasing the ball, and ideally just one touch for more technically advanced players.

COACHING POINTS

Again the aim is to teach midfielders to close down attackers in possession of the ball and the importance of getting close to an opponent. If his opponent plays a wall pass, it is critical that the defender doesn't follow the ball but goes with the runner.

Repeat the drill with red taking the attacking role, and rotate your players.

Once everyone is familiar with the drill, progress so that if midfield defender 1 wins possession he immediately attacks original attacker 1 and tries to run the ball behind him to the opposite end line.

DRILL 43 Competing in the air

PREPARATION Start by marking out one or more areas of 44 x 22 yards (40 x 20m) and position two small goals (approximately 1.75 yards (1.5m) in width), as shown in the diagram. You can use poles or cones if you don't have any small goals.

PLAYERS You will need groups of six players for each marked-out area.

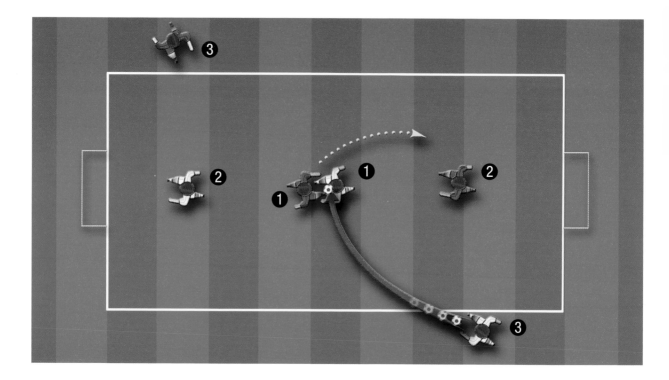

THE DRILL

• White player 3 serves a ball in the air that white and red midfielders 1 compete for. Each is aiming to head the ball on to their respective forwards, i.e. red 1 to red 2 and white 1 to white 2.

• Wherever the ball drops the team that gains possession tries to score in the small goal; however, both forwards must stay in the half in which they started. This can result in a "midfield scuffle" for possession, with the winning player passing the ball to his forward for a shot on goal.

• The forward cannot score directly without first inter-passing with his midfield partner, creating a 2 vs. 1 situation.

• The drill restarts by fighting for the ball that's in the air each time a goal is scored or the ball goes out of bounds. It is important that the servers, who alternate for each play, vary their angle of delivery.

COACHING POINT

Assuming your players all have good heading technique—and if not, have another look at heading skills on pages 46 to 49—then this drill is all about determination and commitment when challenging to win an aerial ball. It encourages players to develop good levels of concentration, the ability to think quickly and have a sharpness about their play.

DRILL 44 Anticipating the knockdowns or rebounds

PREPARATION Start by marking out an area of 44 x 22 yards (40 x 20m) and position two small goals (approximately 1.75 yards (1.5m) in width), as shown in the diagram.

PLAYERS You will need groups of eight players for each marked-out area.

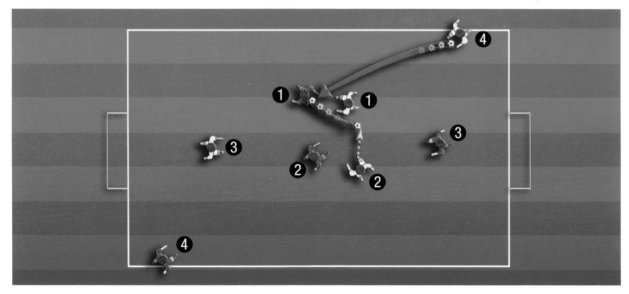

THE DRILL

White player 4 serves a ball in the air that white and red midfielders 1 compete for. Their teammates, white and red players 2, react as the ball drops from whoever has won the aerial battle, trying to gain possession. The team that ultimately gains possession passes the ball to their respective strikers (players numbered 3 on the diagram) creating a 3 vs. 2 situation in the attacking half. As in the previous drill, the forward cannot score directly.

COACHING POINT

The drill will create competition in the air, requiring players to keenly contest the aerial ball and utilize good heading technique to get the ball to their teammates. Then you should see a phase of players fighting for the second ball. It also produces plenty of opportunity for players to close down the opposition, go with runners and practice accurate passing and movement off the ball.

DEFENDING FROM FRONT

DRILL 45 Closing down the opposition/defending from the front

This drill is another designed to encourage players to close down the opposition—in this case forwards who may not instinctively treat this as part of their game.

PREPARATION Mark out an area of 33 x 55 yards (30 x 50m) and position two small goals, as shown in the diagram.

PLAYERS You will need groups of twelve players.

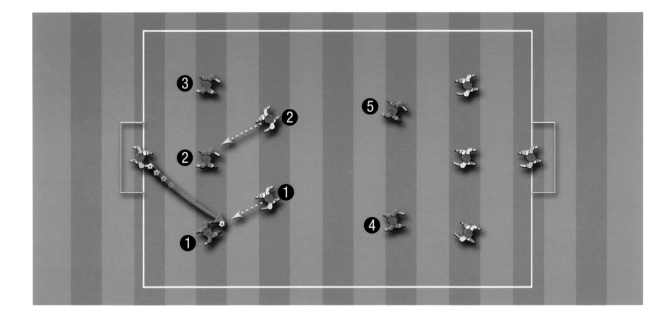

THE DRILL

• The goalkeeper throws the ball out to his defender red player 1. Defending players 2 and 3 must touch the ball before the red team can pass the ball forward to either of their strikers 4 or 5.

• As the red team passes the ball along their defensive line, white players 1 and 2 (who in their advanced position up the pitch are white team's strikers) work to close the ball down, win possession and shoot at the goal.

• If they are unsuccessful, the red team can now pass the ball to their forwards 4 and 5, who attempt to score. Once a shot on goal has been made and the ball is recovered, the drill is restarted by white's goalkeeper, who

throws the ball out to his defenders. Once again all three defenders must touch the ball before attempting to get the ball up to their strikers.

COACHING POINTS

This drill is designed to bring the responsibility of forwards home, to shut down the ball when the opposition has possession in the final third of the field, and to practice key defensive skills such as angles of approach and reducing opposition passing options.

The drill should last for thirty minutes and, unlike many other drills in the book, players assuming the role of strikers should stay as strikers.

MAINTAINING PRESSURE

DRILL 46 Squeezing play

PREPARATION Start by marking out an area of 66 x 44 yards (60 x 40m) and then mark two lines 6 yards (5m) either side of the halfway line, as shown in the diagram.

PLAYERS You will need a group of sixteen players who will be playing an 8 versus 8 game. Both teams will adopt a 3-2-2 formation.

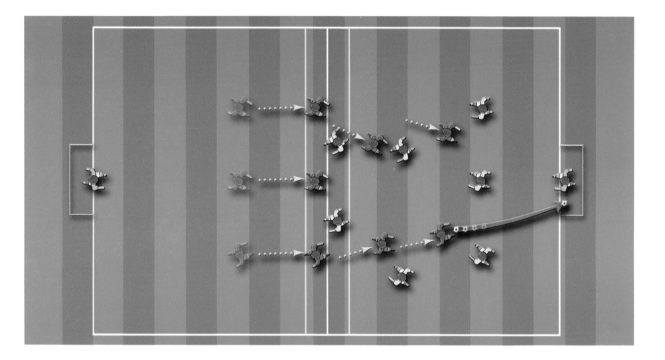

THE GAME

• The game is played in the normal way except that for a goal to count, all of the scoring team (with the exception of the goalkeeper) must be in both the opposition's half and beyond their 5 yard (5m) line. This encourages the attacking team to push up together: in particular the three defenders need to maintain a compact unit. All seven outfield players of the attacking side need to keep team formation and squeeze play into the opposition's half.

• If an attacking team's player doesn't make it beyond the 5 yard (5m) line as his team scores, no goal is given. To even things up, any defending player not retreating quickly enough from the attacking team's half as the attacking team scores causes his team to concede two goals.

COACHING POINTS

The drill, apart from being great fun and a good example of the positive value of peer pressure (pity the slow defending player who gives away an extra goal), promotes excellent levels of concentration and injects a desire in the players to work for the team, especially when defending.

Good defensive values are shown here by the team being compact, pressing play into the opposition half and encouraging a good team ethic.

It is important that the offside rule is rigorously adhered to during the game. You don't want to let bad habits start creeping in.

DEFENDING 1 VS. 1

DRILL 47 Not letting players turn 1

PREPARATION Mark out an area of 33 x 11 yards (30 x 10m) with two "goals" at either end made up of poles placed 1.75 yards (1.5m) apart.

PLAYERS You will need groups of six players for each marked-out area.

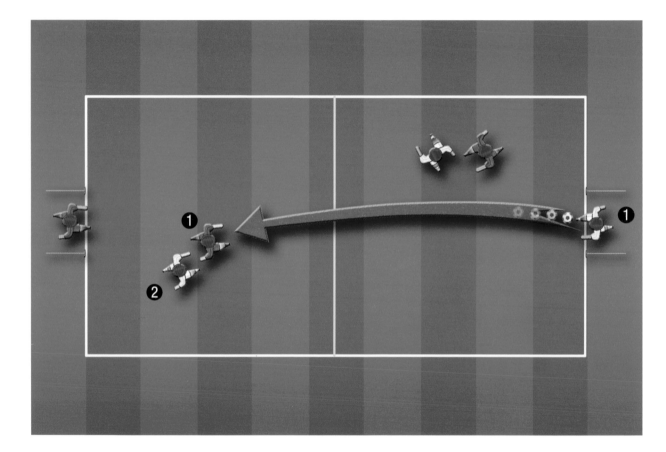

THE DRILL

• White player 1 passes the ball to red player 1, who attempts to turn and pass through the poles to the red target player for a "goal."

• White player 2 moves forward to stop the attacking player turning.

COACHING POINTS

The golden rule for the defender in this situation is to be in a position (touch tight is how it is described)

where he can always see the ball. In other words, he shouldn't be so tight on the attacker that he can't see the ball and can be "rolled" (turned).

The defending player should be constantly trying to force the shielding attacker back toward his own half. Even in the heat of a game, the defender needs to have patience, avoid diving in and must choose his moment to tackle or intercept the ball.

The drill is repeated going in the opposite direction.

DRILL 48 Not letting players turn 2

PREPARATION Start by marking out an area of 44 x 22 yards (40 x 20m). At each end create two goals by placing two poles 1.75 yards (1.5m) apart and 2 yards (2m) in from the corners (see diagram).

PLAYERS You will need a group of ten players.

THE DRILL
• White player 1 starts the drill by passing the ball to red player 2, who tries to turn and pass the ball to red player 1 through either of the two "goals." Red player 2 may exchange passes with his teammate 3 however and whenever he likes.

• It is the job of defending players white 2 and 3 to stop either of the attacking players who are in possession turning with the ball or playing the ball forward to score.

• Once a "goal" is scored, a defending player gains possession or the ball goes out of bounds; the drill is started again from the opposite end.

COACHING POINT
It's important that the defender off the ball, white 3 in this case, takes up a covering position behind his teammate, white 2, who has got tight on his attacker, but is able to get tight on his own attacker if the ball is passed to red 3.

DRILL 49 Marking on crosses 1

PREPARATION The drill is carried out in the penalty area of a full-sized field. You will need two mannequins and a bag of balls.

PLAYERS The drill requires a minimum of seven players, including a goalkeeper.

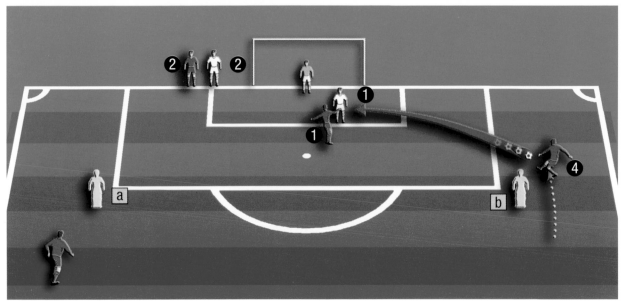

THE DRILL

• Player 4 runs at mannequin b and crosses the ball for attacker red 1. The starting position for the defending player white 1 is all-important: he must mark goal side and in front of red 1.

• As red 4 begins his run and before the delivery of the cross, white 1 must be aware of any movement of red 1,

adjusting his position accordingly. The moment the ball is crossed the defending player must attack the ball with complete determination, heading or volleying the ball clear.

• Give each defender six crosses, then swap the players in the penalty area for the two waiting by the far post. Make sure that all defenders and attackers receive crosses from both the left and right side.

DRILL 50 Marking on crosses 2

PREPARATION The drill is carried out in the penalty area of a full-sized field. You will need two mannequins and a bag of balls.

PLAYERS The drill requires a minimum of nine players, including a goalkeeper.

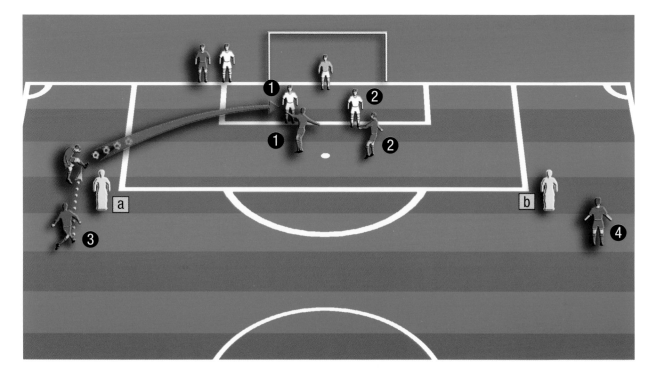

THE DRILL

• The drill is identical to the one on the opposite page, but now we add more players in the penalty box and ask the goalkeeper to play his part in coming for crosses.

• The starting position for the defending players (white 1 and 2) are vital: both should mark goal side and in front of the attackers and must be able to see the ball and their respective attackers.

COACHING POINTS

Winning the battle to be "first to the ball" when dealing with crosses relies on good positioning on the part of the defender. For young players "seeing the ball and the player you are marking" is a particularly difficult concept to grasp as balls are crossed into the penalty area.

The defending player must adopt an open body position and expect the attacker to pull away from the ball, trying to get in behind the defender.

If the defender's position is correct before the cross arrives, and he attacks the ball, it will make it extremely hard for the attacker to get a shot on goal.

It is just as important for the defender not to allow the attacker to run across him and attack the ball.

The aim of the defender is always to be first to the ball.

DRILL 51 1 vs. 1 in wide areas 1

PREPARATION The drill is carried out in half of a full-sized field. The wide areas are sectioned off as shown in the diagram.

PLAYERS The drill requires seven players, including a goalkeeper.

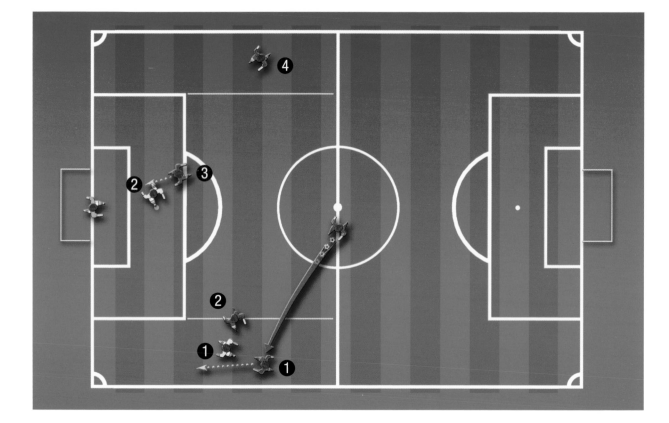

THE DRILL

• The coach starts the drill by passing the ball into the sectioned-off area for attacking player red 1 to try to beat the defender white 1. If red 1 is successful in getting past white 1 (one of his options is to play a wall pass off his teammate red 2), he crosses the ball for red 3 to shoot or head for goal. Defender white 2 now does his best to counter this.

• White 1 can try to intercept the coach's initial pass, but shouldn't go too early or the coach will play a ball in behind him that red 1 can run on to.

• If white 1 can't intercept the first ball, he must get tight on red 1 by taking up a jockeying position showing him the line. Defenders in wide positions like white 1 must learn that if they show their opposition the inside, the attacker may well play a wall pass or come inside to shoot (note: this latter technique is not part of this drill); if red 1 plays a wall pass, the defender must track the run of the player he is marking and not follow the ball.

• Repeat on the right side with white 2 becoming the fullback; red 3 becomes the "wall" and white 1 and red 2 move into the penalty box waiting for the crossed balls.

DRILL 52 1 vs. 1 in wide areas 2

PREPARATION The drill is carried out in half of a full-sized field. The wide areas are sectioned off as shown in the diagram.

PLAYERS The drill requires twelve players, including a goalkeeper.

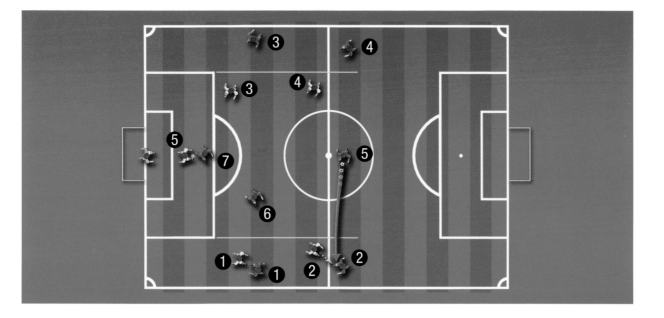

THE DRILL

• Red 5 starts the drill, playing the ball to red 2. Red players 2 and 1 try to get down the line to cross the ball for red 7, who is marked by white 5. Red 1 can use red 6 for a wall pass (as described in the drill on the opposite page).

• White 2 must close down red 2 by taking up a jockeying position and showing him "back inside," shutting off the pass to red 1.

• If red 5 senses, before he releases his pass, that white 2 has reduced red 2's options by getting close, then he can change the play by passing to red 4 on his right instead. The wide ball scenario will now evolve with white 4 reacting to the pass and attempting to show red 4 "back inside." Red 2 or 4 can pass back to red 5, who can change the play as he sees it.

• Sooner or later the ball will go down the line to either red 1 or 3, and it's then up to white players 1 or 3 to work him forward down the line. If either red player 2 or 4 go on an overlapping run beyond red 1 or 3, white players 2 or 4 must track the runner to prevent damaging crosses.

COACHING POINTS

This is a high tempo drill that introduces the elements of defensive marking and covering. Players must consistently "press" the player with the ball, track any forward movement of the attacking side, move to cover positions when defending players track runners, and learn to anticipate the buildup of dangerous and threatening attacking play.

White players 1, 2, 3 or 4 cannot go into the wide areas before the ball is passed in.

GROUP DEFENDING

DRILL 53 Defensive marking and covering

PREPARATION Mark out an area 44 x 22 yards (40 x 20m) plus 2 yard (2m) end zones, as shown in the diagram.

PLAYERS The drill requires twelve players.

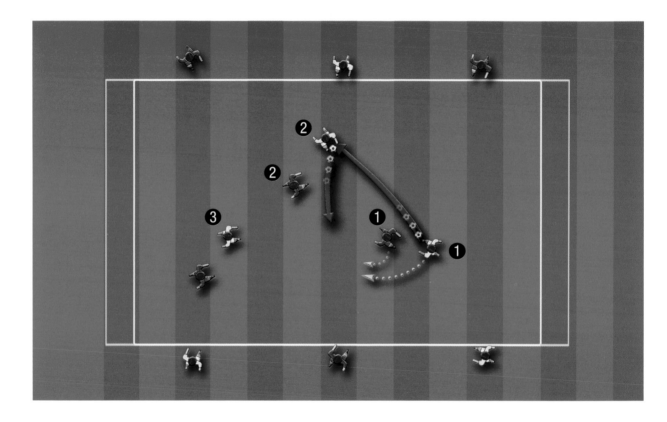

THE DRILL

• The drill requires both teams to defend an end zone. In order to score, either team must run into the opposition's end zone with the ball or receive a pass as they cross into the end zone. It should go without saying that for obvious reasons no player can "goal hang" by waiting in the end zone, and it is feasible (and desirable) to play to the offside rule.

• The drill begins as white 1 passes to white 2 and runs forward to receive the return pass. Red 2 must close down white 2 and stop him turning; red 1 must track the run of white 1 to stop him receiving the ball back.

• The players on the sides can only "play" for their own team: whites to whites, reds to reds and, in addition, may only take a maximum of two touches.

• If the drill is carried out at the right tempo, you will need to substitute your teams after five minutes or so.

COACHING POINT

Even in this simple drill good defensive principles must be adopted by all players: they should press the players on the ball, track any forward movement and cover each other. Players should always anticipate dangerous movement on the part of the opposition.

DRILL 54 Defending as a team

PREPARATION The drill is carried out on two-thirds of a full-sized field.

PLAYERS The drill requires sixteen players plus a goalkeeper. The defensive set-up consists of a goalkeeper, a back four and a midfield three. In fact, we ask the midfield three to play as if they had a fourth team member on the field. We do this because we actually want problematic defensive situations to arise.

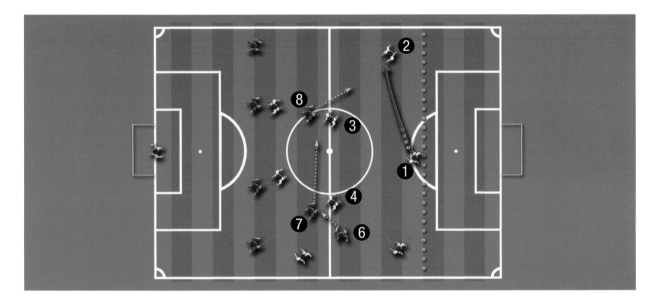

THE DRILL

• Now we put it all together. In this drill we ask the players to defend the middle and defensive thirds of the field.

• In the diagram the white team is attacking red team's goal. White 1 has the ball and passes it to white 2. As the ball is passed, defending midfielder red 8 leaves white 3 and moves toward white 2; red 7 moves to his left to mark white 3, and red 6 moves over to mark white 4; red 8 takes up a marking position showing white 2 back inside.

COACHING POINTS

All the critical components of successful defensive play practiced earlier now come into play: keeping the team compact; closing down the player with the ball to limit their passing opportunities; tracking any forward runs; and constant and good communication between teammates. Above all players must show real team effort and a habit of working for each other.

The scenario shown consists of nine white players versus seven outfield red players. White 1 becomes a server only, and by adopting all of the previously described defending principles the defending reds should cope well with most of the situations that arise. It is important when working the team that the defenders understand that it is the central defenders who dictate how high or deep the back line should be: when they push up or drop off the fullbacks follow.

As a general rule the fullbacks should not be deeper than the centerback; they should be at least level. If not you will not have a compact unit of players and mistakes and misunderstandings can occur.

ATTACKING PLAY

During matches the accuracy of crosses is critical: well-executed crosses enable receiving players to attack the ball and head for goal. In fact, a team that underestimates the importance of heading as an attacking skill will considerably lessen the potency of their striking force. In this section we are concentrating on the heading action itself. One final point—heading should be practiced, with the emphasis on correct technique, from a young age to eliminate any fears or hesitancy.

DRILL 55 Heading at the near post

PREPARATION The drill is carried out in the penalty box of a full-sized field. You will need a mannequin.

PLAYERS Ten players plus a goalkeeper.

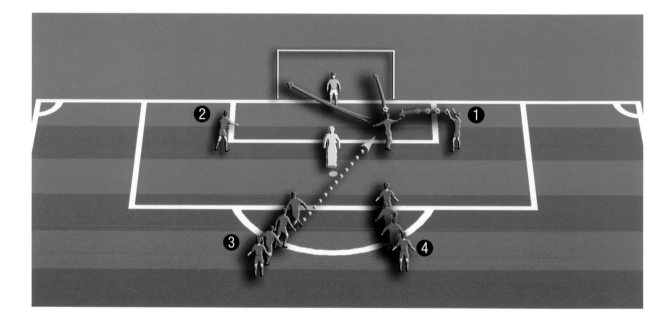

THE DRILL

• Player 1 serves underarm to player 3, who is running into the near-post area. The ball should be served into the space behind and to the left of the mannequin. Player 3 must attack the ball and head for goal, either by heading into the space to the left of the goalkeeper or across the goalkeeper and into the space to his right.

• Once all the players in the lines have had several tries, players 3 and 4 become the servers and players 1 and 2 join the line. It is important that all players practice their runs on both the right and left sides. Using a mannequin will encourage attacking players to get across defenders.

COACHING POINT

The heading player, with eyes firmly on the ball, must attack both the space and the ball, and head on the run. The focus of this drill is on the timing of each player's run and the technique of heading the ball. At this stage we are not asking players to jump for the ball. An alternative to the standard drill is to use a lower serve and encourage diving headers at the near post.

DRILL 56 Heading at the far post

PREPARATION The drill is carried out in the penalty box of a full-sized field. You will need two mannequins and a pole.

PLAYERS Eight players plus a goalkeeper.

THE DRILL

• The server, player 1, volleys the ball from his hands high to the far post. Player 2 makes his run from the pole, gets behind the mannequin on the left and, using a one-footed take-off, heads for the goal, either across the goalkeeper to the far post or inside the near post. Player 2 swaps places with player 1 to act as server and player 1 joins the line. The drill is repeated on the left side, starting with player 3 serving to player 4. During this drill we ask the goalkeeper not to come for the crossed ball.

COACHING POINTS

You are encouraging players to keep their eyes on the ball and to head the ball at the top of their jump—players should have a slightly arched back and head through the ball.

Eventually you will want to progress, using defenders to put pressure on the attacking players (as in the next drill), but this is only possible once the players are technically proficient crossers and headers of the ball.

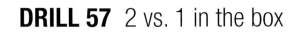

DRILL 57 2 vs. 1 in the box

PREPARATION The drill is carried out in the penalty box of a full-sized field. You will need two mannequins.

PLAYERS Eight players plus a goalkeeper.

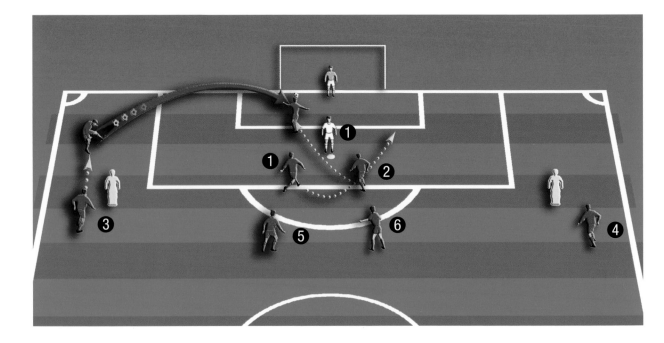

THE DRILL

• Player 3 runs past the mannequin and crosses the ball into the box; before the cross comes in, players 1 and 2 make crossover runs, with player 1 pulling away to the far post in anticipation of a high cross, and player 2 running across the defender white 1 to the space on the near post. In the diagram the ball is crossed to the near post for attacking player red 2 to head for the goal.

• To begin with we ask defender white 1 to stay passive, but once you are confident that your players have developed a reasonable standard of crossing and heading, then you should add to the realism by asking the defender to defend the crosses properly. Throughout the drill the goalkeeper must only come for crosses in the six-yard box.

• After the cross has been headed (or the defender has won the ball) the drill is repeated on the other side of the field with player 4 making his run past the mannequin. Players 1 and 2 rejoin the line and 5 and 6 step up to the edge of the penalty box ready to make their crossover runs. Replace the defender periodically.

If the drill does not move on to using an "active" defender, replace the player with a mannequin.

COACHING POINT

The player making the cross must lift his head before crossing the ball and mentally note the positions of the defender and his two attacking teammates. Only when he has a clear picture of the position and movement of the players in the box should he decide on the type and placement of the cross he is about to execute.

TURNING AND SHOOTING

Forwards spend a good deal of time during games with their backs to goal. Players that can effectively hold up and shield the ball from closing defenders, then quickly turn and shoot, will reap huge rewards.

DRILL 58 Back foot turn and shoot

PREPARATION The drill is carried around the penalty box of a full-sized field.

PLAYERS Six forwards plus a goalkeeper.

THE DRILL

• Player 3 passes to player 1 who "comes off" the mannequin to perform a back-foot turn (see ball mastery on page 30). Immediately after he turns he pushes the ball forward and to his right and shoots at the goal right footed. Speed of execution of the turn and shot are vital.

• Player 1 retrieves his ball and rejoins the line as players 2 and 4 repeat the drill on the right side of the field.

COACHING POINTS

This drill is all about the attacking player's turn. You are looking at the accuracy and efficiency of the turn, especially the placement of the ball for the second touch, which will be all-important when it comes to getting away the shot.

The less space the forward needs to perform the turn and shot, the more effective he will become.

Note that from the left side it is a right-footed turn and shot and vice versa from the right.

This drill is an excellent simulation of creating space to "come off" a defender and turning him, which is a vital skill for every striker.

DRILL 59 Shield, fake, turn and shoot

PREPARATION The drill is carried out around the penalty box of a full-sized field.

PLAYERS Ten players: six forwards, four defenders plus a goalkeeper.

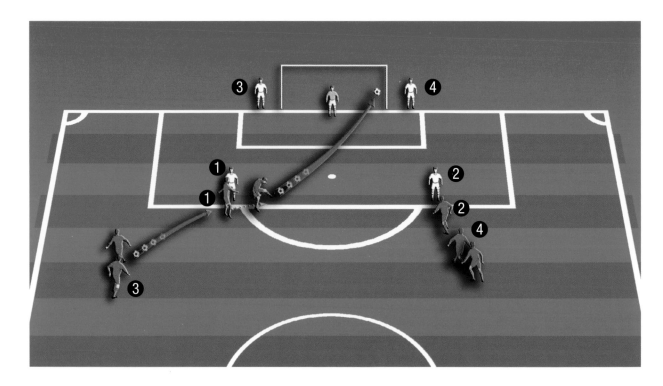

THE DRILL

• Attacking red player 3 passes to player 1, who is being tightly marked by white defender 1. Attacker player 1 positions his body on the half-turn and receives the ball with the outside of the front foot, i.e. the foot that is farthest from the defender (right foot in the diagram) at the same time he is holding the defender off with his left side. The attacker now brings the inside of his left foot over the ball and plants it on the ground; with his weight on his left foot, he uses his right foot to push the ball inside the defender and turns and shoots right-footed.

• In this drill we ask the defender to stay passive after he has initially pressed the attacker as he receives the ball and not interfere with the turn and the shot. We want the attacking player to learn to feel the presence of the defender.

• Player 1 gets his ball and rejoins the line and the drill is repeated on the opposite side, using players numbered 2 and 4. Defenders 1 and 2 change with 3 and 4 after three tries each.

COACHING POINT

During this drill the attacking players are attempting a classic fake and its success will depend on the speed of execution and the quality of their turns. Be sure players are comfortable performing the technique before introducing them to this drill. You may need to practice using mannequins before introducing defenders.

ATTACKING CROSSES

Movement in and around the penalty area unlocks defenses, but timing is the key. These drills will help players avoid the offside trap and arrive in the right place at the right time to meet the crossed ball.

DRILL 60 Diagonal cross behind the defense from deep

PREPARATION The drill is carried out around the penalty box of a full-sized field. You will need six mannequins.

PLAYERS Six or more players plus a goalkeeper.

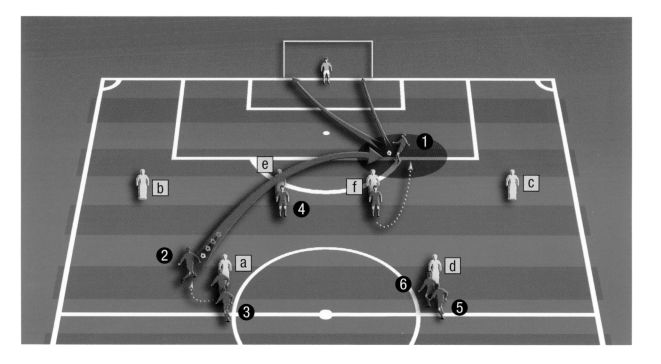

THE DRILL

• Player 2 moves the ball to the left of mannequin a and crosses with his left foot diagonally over and behind mannequin f (into the area shaded in the diagram). Player 1 starts the drill in front of mannequin f, but, just as the ball is about to be crossed, moves away and looks to get in behind it. He controls the pass and shoots at the goal. To simulate a game situation, the striker's run must be timed so that he receives the lofted pass from an onside position.

• Throughout the drill, players 2, 3, 5 and 6 continue to cross the ball and players 1 and 4 stay as strikers.

• The drill is repeated on the opposite side. Note, naturally left-footed players should perform the drill on the left side of the pitch and vice versa.

COACHING POINTS

This drill is designed to improve a number of key skills: crossing the ball accurately, timing runs, controlling lofted passes and developing the composure of forwards to execute quality finishes. The accuracy of the diagonal cross is the key factor.

The coach must ensure his players always play to the offside rule.

DRILL 61 Near-post cross and run

PREPARATION The drill is carried out around the penalty box of a full-sized field. You will need four mannequins. Note, in the diagram the two central mannequins are "squeezed" together to encourage the strikers to make near-post runs.

PLAYERS Six or more players plus a goalkeeper.

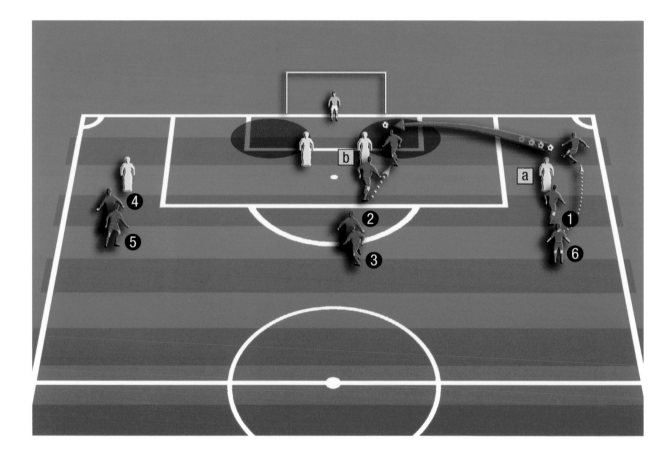

THE DRILL

• Player 1 pushes the ball to the side and just behind mannequin a, then crosses the ball into the shaded area behind and to the side of mannequin b. Player 2 makes his run into the shaded area before player 1 crosses. The ideal cross will be below head height and if the crossed ball is low player 2 must guide it with his foot (probably his right) into the goal. If the cross is off the ground then he will either volley or head the ball at the goal.

• The drill is repeated on the opposite side. Players 2 and 3 remain as strikers, players 4, 5 and 6 remain as crossers of the ball.

COACHING POINT

Again you are looking for accuracy of the crosses, timing of the run to the near post and the striker making good contact on the cross as he finishes. Power on the shot or header is not normally required this close to the goal.

DRILL 62 Far-post cross and run

PREPARATION The drill is carried out around the penalty box of a full-sized field. You will need four mannequins.

PLAYERS Six or more players plus a goalkeeper. Six or more balls.

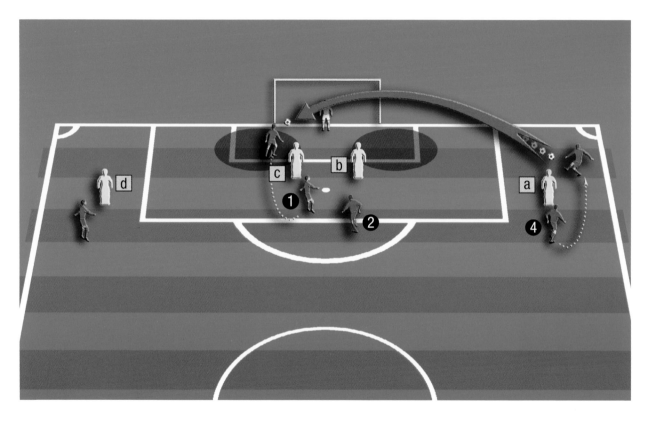

THE DRILL

• Player 4 pushes the ball past mannequin a, while simultaneously player 1 "pulls away" from mannequin c and toward the far post; he is now in space and facing the direction of the cross. Player 1's momentum should make it possible for him to take a run at the ball, gaining plenty of height from his one-footed take-off. His run should also have taken him into the blind side of mannequin c.

• Before crossing the ball player 4 must look up to assess the positions of player 1 and the goalkeeper. Once he has a clear mental picture of the position and movement of the players in the penalty box, he crosses the ball high into the shaded area in front of the far post, eliminating the goalkeeper and mannequin c, and delivering a ball that allows player 1 to climb high and head for the goal.

• During the drill we ask the goalkeeper to make saves but not come for the crossed ball.

COACHING POINT
This drill is all about the accuracy of the crosses, getting them into the right area and at the right height. The strikers must be determined, making well-timed and angled runs and meeting each cross with a firm, well-directed header.

DRILL 63 2 vs. 1 in the box

Now we introduce defenders in place of mannequins, who will provide much more of a test for the strikers. Once the strikers succeed in getting the better of the defenders during the drill their confidence will grow, which should carry over to match situations. During the drill always make sure that the forwards outnumber the defenders.

PREPARATION The drill is carried out around the penalty box of a full-sized field. You will need two mannequins.

PLAYERS Ten players plus a goalkeeper.

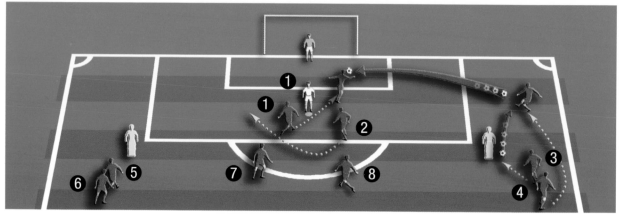

THE DRILL

• We start the drill by creating movement to help the timing of the strikers' runs; attacking player 3 passes into space for overlapping player 4 to cross the ball.

• As the movement is developing, attacking players 1 and 2 are on the move, trying to lose the marking of defender player 1.

• In the diagram player 4 crosses to the near-post area, where player 1 has made his run; player 2 has pulled away to the far post to attack a possible far-post cross.

• Change the defender periodically: attackers 1 and 2 alternate with 7 and 8 and players 3 and 4 plus 5 and 6 remain crossing balls.

RUNNING FORWARD FROM MIDFIELD

A player running from the midfield, off the ball, and getting in behind the defending back line can be devastatingly effective. Difficult to mark and usually on the blind side of the defenders who are concentrating on the ball, the run often produces a shot on goal.

Midfield players need to practice the timing of their runs to avoid being frequently caught offside.

DRILL 64 Pass square and run forward (central)

PREPARATION The drill is carried out on half of the field, and you will need a good supply of balls and two mannequins.

PLAYERS Six players plus a goalkeeper.

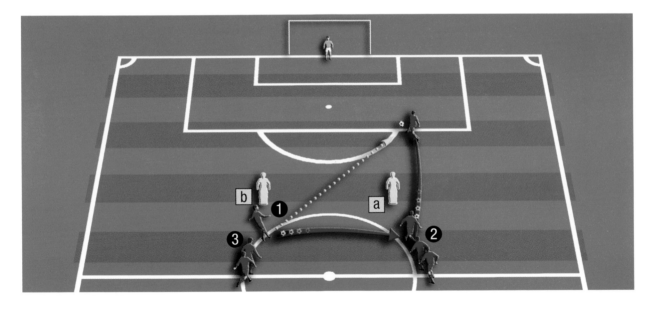

THE DRILL

• Player 1 passes the ball square to player 2 and makes a forward run diagonally behind mannequin a.

• Player 2 takes two touches: first his controlling touch is with the inside of his right foot, leaving the ball playable in front and slightly to his right side and facing the goal; his second touch, which needs to be carefully weighted, passes the ball down the side and behind mannequin a.

• Player 1 must time his run to avoid being "offside" and player 2's pass must not run through to the goalkeeper.

• Player 1 controls the ball he receives from player 2 and shoots at the goal. After retrieving his ball player 1 rejoins the back of the line of his waiting teammates.

• Player 2 now passes his ball to player 3 and the drill is repeated on the left side of the field with player 2 running diagonally behind mannequin b.

DRILL 65 Pass square and run forward (wide area)

PREPARATION The drill is carried out on half of the field and you will need six balls and four mannequins.

PLAYERS Nine players plus a goalkeeper.

THE DRILL

• Player 1 passes the ball square to "wide" player 2 who, with two touches as described in the previous drill, passes the ball into the run of player 1, who in the meantime has run forward and diagonally into space behind mannequin d. Player 1 crosses the ball first time for player 5 who shoots at the goal—the technique player

5 uses to shoot depends on the quality and type of cross player 1 makes. Player 5 rejoins the line on the right.

• The drill is repeated on the left side of the field as player 3 passes to player 4, player 3 runs diagonally behind mannequin a, player 4 passes the ball into the run of player 3, who crosses to player 1, who has replaced player 5.

DRILL 66 Arriving late in the box

PREPARATION The drill is carried out on half of the field and you will need six balls and two mannequins.

PLAYERS Eight players plus a goalkeeper.

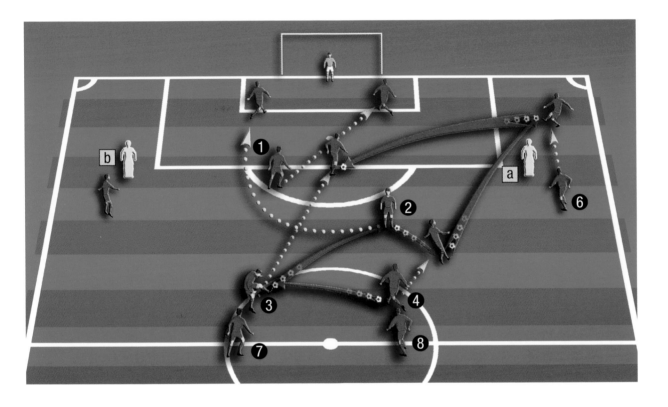

THE DRILL

• Player 4 passes to player 3, who in turn passes first time to player 2 (striker). Player 4 takes up a position to receive a first-time "lay off" from player 2. Midfield player 4 passes inside mannequin a for player 6 to run on to and cross the ball. Player 1 makes an early run to the near post in anticipation of player 6's cross. Player 2, after passing to player 4, spins away to take up a position on the far post.

• Midfield player 3 makes a forward run into the center of the box (penalty area), arriving later and behind the runs of players 1 and 2. The wide player 6 tries to pick out the late run of player 3 for him to score.

• Players 3 and 4 now become the strikers; players 7 and 8 the midfield pair and players 1 and 2 rejoin the line of waiting players.

• The sequence repeats with player 7 passing to player 8 and the drill is performed down the left side of the field.

COACHING POINT

You are looking for weight and accuracy of passing, timing of runs, accuracy of crosses and the quality of the finishing. This drill should be carried out at a good tempo. Advance the drill by adding defenders to increase the difficulty.

EXPLOITING 2 vs. 1 IN WIDE AREAS

During games attacking players are always trying to create a situation where two attackers confront one defender (2 vs. 1), usually in the attacking third of the field. These moments often break down, handing the advantage back to the defending team. The following drills focus on how speed, communication and timing of the final pass in 2 vs. 1 situations can be improved.

DRILL 67 Using the wingers' space

PREPARATION The drill is carried out on half of the field. You will need six balls and four mannequins.

PLAYERS Eight players plus a goalkeeper.

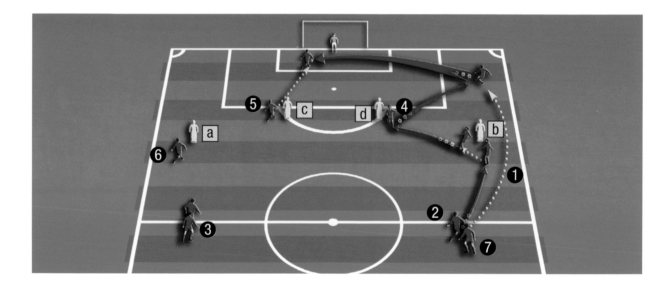

THE DRILL

• Player 2 passes to player 1, who turns to face mannequin b, which represents a defender. Player 1 runs with the ball inside and passes to player 4 (striker): meanwhile player 2 has carried his run forward overlapping player 1 on the outside and into the space behind mannequin b.

• Player 4 passes, either first time or with a controlling touch, into the run of player 2, who crosses for player 5 who, in turn, attacks the space behind mannequin c to meet the crossed ball.

• Player 2 becomes player 1, player 1 joins the line and player 7 becomes player 2. Player 4 remains as striker, who will attack the crossed ball when the drill is repeated on the left side with players 3, 6 and 5.

COACHING POINT

Again you are looking for weight and accuracy of passes, good timing of the runs and quality and accuracy of the final crossed ball which enables the striker to shoot cleanly for the goal. This drill should be carried out at a fast tempo and with good energy levels.

DRILL 68 Developing width in attack

PREPARATION The game is played on three-quarters of a field with one of the goals set up on the edge of the box. You will need sufficient disks to mark up the wide areas as shown.

PLAYERS Twenty players, including two goalkeepers. If you do not have twenty players then you should adapt the size of the "field" accordingly.

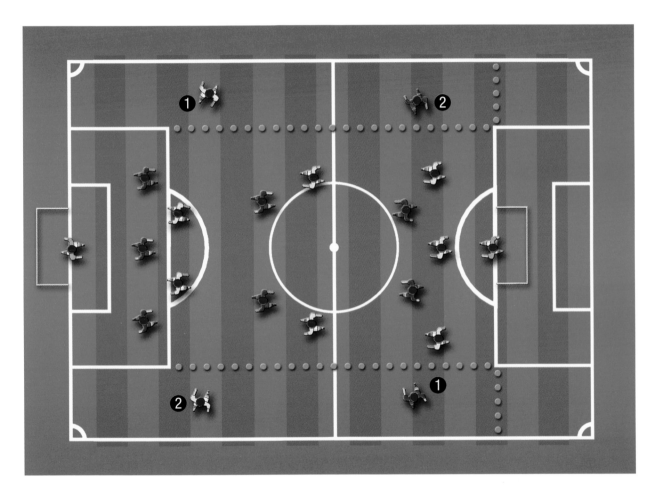

THE DRILL (GAME)

• The idea of the game is that each side tries to pass the ball wide to either red or white players 1 and 2. The only players that cannot pass to the wide players are the goalkeepers.

• No players are allowed into the wide areas until the ball has been passed in to the attacking players 1 and 2, who always stay inside the marked-off wide areas. At this point one defending player and one attacking player are permitted in the wide area, creating a 2 vs. 1 situation.

• Note that the natural halfway line of the field is not the central point of the practice area.

• The drill stresses the need for width when attacking.

DRILL 69 Advanced overlapping game

PREPARATION As Drill 68.

PLAYERS Twenty players, including two goalkeepers. If you do not have twenty players then you should adapt the size of the "field" accordingly.

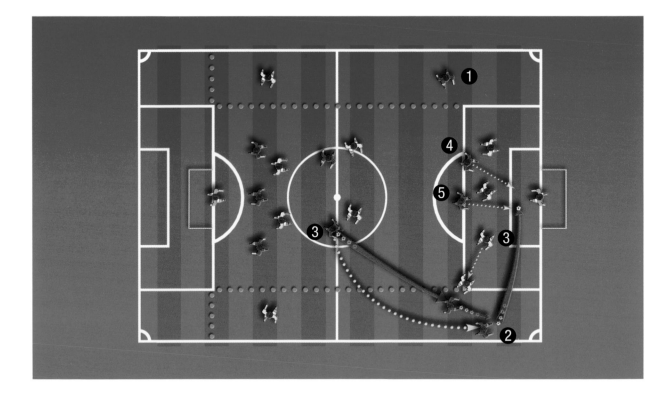

THE DRILL (GAME)

• The game is set up with the same rules as for the previous game. Once the ball has been passed successfully into a wide area, and a 2 vs. 1 against the defending team exists, it is up to the attacking players to exploit the situation by first creating an overlap and then crossing the ball into the goal area for their strikers to attack.

• In the diagram, attacking red player 3 has the ball and passes wide to red player 2, defender white player 3 runs into the wide area to put pressure on the attacker. Red player 3 also runs wide in support of red player 2, creating a 2 vs. 1 against defender white player 3.

• Red player 2 passes to red player 3 as he overlaps, who now crosses for red players 4 and 5 to attack.

• These types of play will be created in all four wide areas of the field, regularly bringing about 2 vs. 1 situations. As the players begin to understand the game, you can allow the far wide players (red player 1 in the diagram) to attack the far post as red player 3 crosses the ball.

COACHING POINT
The game should be played at a good tempo with excellent communication between the players, who should demonstrate good awareness as play develops and show lots of enthusiasm.

TURNING THE OPPOSITION

This is all about learning to exploit the space behind the defenders and, at the same time, creating uncertainty in the minds of defenders—will the ball be played to the feet of the attacker or into the space behind the defender for the attacker to run on to?

DRILL 70 Come short and spin

PREPARATION The drill is carried out on half of the field and you will need two mannequins.

PLAYERS Eight or more players plus a goalkeeper.

THE DRILL

• Player 1 passes the ball square to player 2, whose first touch is with the inside of his right foot. This will leave the ball playable just in front of him and to his right.

• As player 2 controls the received ball, and before he plays his pass, player 3 moves slightly toward the ball. At the moment player 2's head dips as he begins his passing action, player 3 spins away showing and calling where he wants the ball (in this case behind and to the outside of mannequin a).

• Player 3 spins on to the ball, running to the edge of the box to shoot at the goal. Player 4 also runs in behind, looking to score from any rebounds from the goalkeeper.

• Players 3 and 4 rejoin the line and players 1 and 2 move up to the mannequins. The drill is repeated on the left.

DRILL 71 Set-up and run in behind

PREPARATION The drill is carried out on half of the field and you will need two mannequins.

PLAYERS Eight or more players plus a goalkeeper.

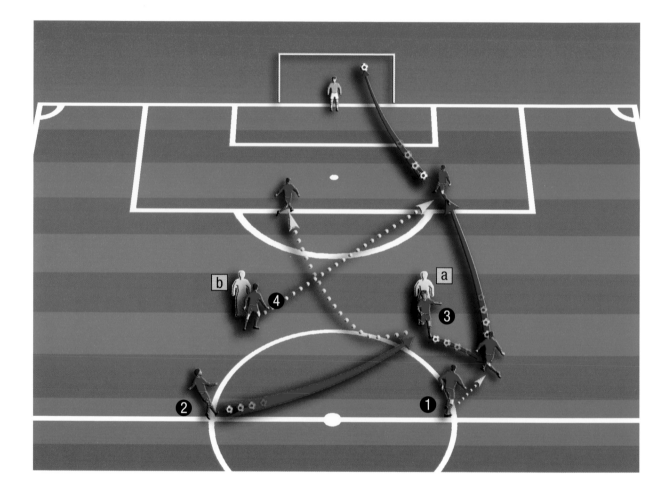

THE DRILL

• Player 2 passes diagonally to player 3, who then comes short of mannequin a and sets the ball back to player 1, who has made a passing angle to the right.

• As player 1 prepares to pass the ball, player 4, anticipating a pass, makes a diagonal run behind mannequin a. Player 1 sees the run and passes the ball in to space for player 4 to run on to.

• Player 3 spins away in the opposite direction to support player 4. Player 4 shoots if he is central or crosses square for player 3 if player 1's pass is too wide. Player 3 must ensure that he is always behind the ball to avoid an offside situation.

• Players 1 and 2 become players 3 and 4, other players in the waiting line move up to become players 1 and 2 and the original 3 and 4 rejoin the line. The drill is repeated in the left side.

RUNNING AT DEFENDERS

Running with the ball has become something of a lost art, which is a pity; coaches should encourage it whenever the opportunity arises. When done well it creates real unease among defenders, making them backpedal.

DRILL 72 Run inside to commit defender

PREPARATION The drill is carried out on half of the field and you will need four mannequins.

PLAYERS Ten players plus a goalkeeper.

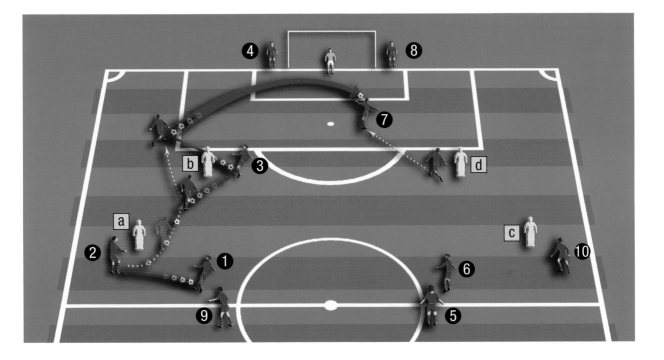

THE DRILL

• Player 1 passes wide to player 2, who pushes the ball inside mannequin a and runs at mannequin b. Player 3, who is being "marked" by mannequin b, pulls to the left side of the mannequin.

• In a game situation the defender, simulated by mannequin b, would know how potentially dangerous the direct run of player 2 could be. Player 2 passes inside to player 3, who in turn passes first time with the inside of his right foot to the continuing run of player 2 behind mannequin b.

• Player 2 crosses left-footed for player 7 to attack. The drill is repeated on the right side.

• Players 1, 2 and 9 alternate roles as do players 5, 6 and 10. Players 3 and 4 should alternate periodically as should players 7 and 8.

COACHING POINT

You are looking for speed of movement—players must run with the ball at pace, keeping it within playing distance. Passes need to be accurate. Maintain a good flow and tempo throughout the drill.

DRILL 73 Committing the last defender

PREPARATION The drill is carried out on half of the field, which is coned off so that only the width of the penalty box can be used. You will need one mannequin.

PLAYERS Eight players plus a goalkeeper.

THE DRILL

• Player 1 passes square to player 2, who passes first time using the inside of his right foot to the right and behind the mannequin. Player 1 makes a diagonal run behind the mannequin and receives the return pass.

• Without breaking his stride he immediately runs with the ball at the defending white player 1. Attacking player 2, having made his pass to player 1, runs behind player 1 and in front of the mannequin, giving support to player 1 and creating a 2 vs. 1 against the defender.

• Attacking player 1 now has two options: (1) to run directly at the goal, taking on the defender and shooting

for the goal, or (2) he draws the defender to the ball and passes to player 2, who now goes forward and shoots. Player 2 must not go behind defender white player 1, or he will have taken up an offside position.

• After the shot at the goal attacking players 1 and 2 rejoin the line, and other players waiting in line repeat the drill. Defending player 1 is replaced by player 2.

• It is important that the defender tries hard throughout the drill to stop the attackers from scoring. Encourage competitiveness, but be aware that it can be an exhausting role as a lone defender and they will need to be changed regularly to maintain the quality of play.

CREATIVE MOVEMENT AROUND THE BOX

Creating space and goal-scoring opportunities in and around the penalty box is difficult—it is the most defended and keenly contested area of the field. Skilful use of fake moves and sleight of foot can create openings and unlock the defense. During these drills encourage your players to experiment and have fun, and to keep up a good tempo.

DRILL 74 "Take over," pass, cross and finish 1

PREPARATION The drill is carried out on half of the field and you will need two mannequins.

PLAYERS Eight or more players plus a goalkeeper.

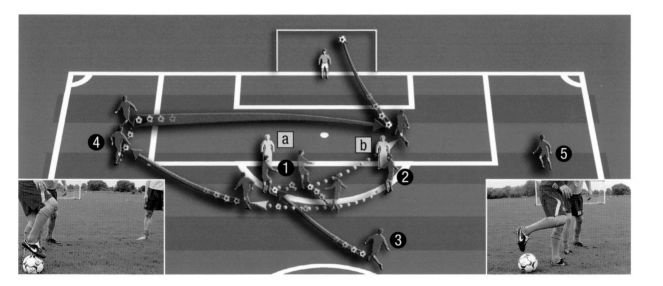

THE DRILL

• Player 3 passes to the feet of player 1, who controls the ball with his right foot and with his body on the half-turn facing player 2.

• Player 1 runs the ball toward player 2 more or less along the edge of the penalty area; simultaneously player 2 runs toward player 1. As they are about to cross over—with player 2 on player 1's right side—player 1 rolls the ball with the sole of his foot into the path of player 2.

• Player 2 receives the ball and passes it wide to player 4, who crosses the ball for player 1, who has carried on his run into the box. Player 1 attempts to score.

• Player 3 replaces player 1 and starts at mannequin a, player 2 goes to mannequin b and it is player 2 who receives the ball at his feet from the next player waiting in line.

• The drill is repeated in the opposite direction with player 5 crossing for player 2. Players 4 and 5 stay wide crossing balls and the central players interchange one at a time. Speed and the timing of the exchange of passes are the keys to making this drill realistic.

DRILL 75 "Take over," pass, cross and finish 2

An alternative way of playing out the drill is for player 1 to offer a dummy at the point of crossover, taking the ball on and shooting at the goal The dummy takes the form of a deceiving movement: player 1 acts as if to roll the ball back with the sole of the foot to player 2, who uses his run as a diversion. Player 1 continues with the ball and goes to shoot at the goal.

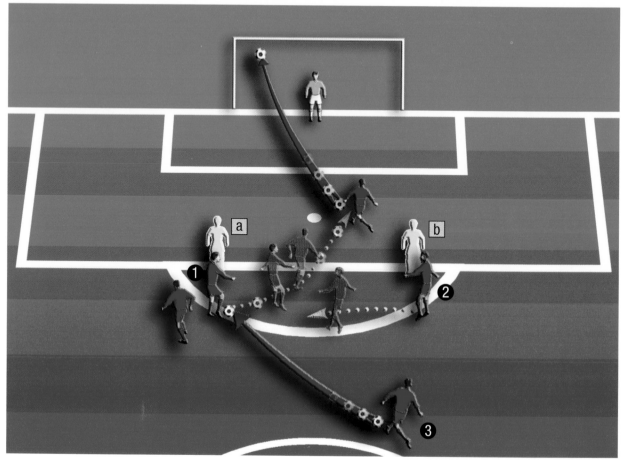

DRILL 76 Fake, spin and shoot

PREPARATION The drill is carried out on half of the field and you will need three mannequins.

PLAYERS Seven or more players plus a goalkeeper.

THE DRILL

• Player 1 passes to player 2, who moves toward the ball. Instead of controlling or passing the ball, player 2 fakes playing the ball and lets it run on. Player 3, who anticipates player 2's disguise, is ready to play a first-time pass behind mannequin a.

• Player 2, after his dummy move, turns quickly and runs past mannequin a to receive player 3's pass. Player 2 controls the ball and shoots at the goal. He might be able to shoot the first time if player 3's pass is correctly weighted.

• Player 3 stays in the central position (he can be replaced periodically). Player 2 retrieves his ball and rejoins the line on the right. Player 1 moves up to mannequin a and the drill is repeated on the left with the players waiting in line.

COACHING POINT

During this drill you are looking for accurately weighted passes, good speed of movement and accurate shooting. And insist that the players make the fake moves look as realistic as possible!

BLIND-SIDE RUNS

A blind-side run takes an off-the-ball player behind defenders who are facing and concentrating on the player with the ball. When it works, the player making the run arrives unopposed in space behind the defensive line, onside and in a threatening position. It takes skill on the part of the passing player to recognize the situation as it develops and to time and weight his pass to the running player.

DRILL 77 Running on the blind side centrally

PREPARATION The drill is carried out on half of the field. You will need four mannequins.

PLAYERS Eight or more players plus a goalkeeper.

THE DRILL

• Player 1 runs with the ball up to mannequin a as player 2 makes a diagonal run on the "blind side" of the same mannequin. Player 1 passes the ball into space behind and to mannequin a's left side. Player 2 picks up the ball and keeps running diagonally toward mannequin d.

• Player 3 starts to run diagonally on to the blind side of mannequin d. Player 2 picks out the run of player 3 by playing the ball into space behind and to the right of mannequin d; player 3 now goes on to shoot at the goal.

• Player 3's run and player 2's pass must be accurately timed and paced so that player 3 does not run "offside," and the through pass into space does not give the goalkeeper a chance to collect.

• Player 2 becomes player 3, player 1 becomes player 2 and player 3 rejoins the line. The drill is repeated on the other side starting with player 4 waiting in line, who runs the ball toward mannequin b.

DRILL 78 Running on the blind side in wide areas

PREPARATION The drill is carried out on half of the field. You will need four mannequins.

PLAYERS Ten players plus a goalkeeper.

THE DRILL

• Player 1 runs diagonally with the ball toward mannequin a, player 2 runs on the blind side of mannequin a, player 1 passes into the run of player 2, behind and to the left of mannequin a.

• Player 2 picks the ball up and runs toward mannequin b and passes into the space that player 3 is running into behind and down the right side of mannequin b.

• Player 3 must time his run to avoid being "offside." When player 3 collects the pass, he quickly crosses left-footed into the run of the waiting striker player 8.

• Player 1 becomes player 2, player 2 becomes player 3. Player 3 rejoins the line (players 7 and 8 stay as permanent strikers).

• The drill is repeated on the right, starting with the players waiting in line.

COACHING POINT

This drill is all about the pace of the passes, timing of the players' runs and good vocal communication between players. The drill must be carried out at a good match-paced tempo, but limit the players to two touches on the ball to help aid timing and execution of the passes.

COUNTERATTACKING

Counterattacking, or attacking on the break, is now a common sight in top-level soccer. These days many midfield players are the possessors of superb defending skills and once they've broken up an attack and gained possession, quickly exploit the space left behind the attacking team, who are momentarily disorganized and probably outnumbered.

DRILL 79 3 vs. 2 counterattack

PREPARATION The drill is carried out on half of the field.

PLAYERS Nine players plus a goalkeeper.

THE DRILL
• Defender white player 2 attempts to pass to defender white player 3.

• Attacking red player 2 intercepts and immediately passes the ball to striker player 1, who is being marked by defending player 1.

• Wide attacking players 3 and 4 break quickly to support player 1, while defender player 2 retreats quickly to help win the ball back.

• This will create a situation of three attacking players (1, 3 and 4) confronting two defenders (1 and 2), one of whom is still recovering.

• The attackers try to create a goal-scoring opportunity before the defense can recover. Speed of attack is essential.

DRILL 80 "Break out" to score

PREPARATION The drill is carried out on a full field. Mark an area of 33 x 33 yards (30 x 30m) with disks around the center circle. Four players from each side are in the marked-off area. Defender 2 marks attacker 1 just outside the penalty area at one end and defender 2 marks attacker 1 at the other end.

PLAYERS Twelve players plus two goalkeepers.

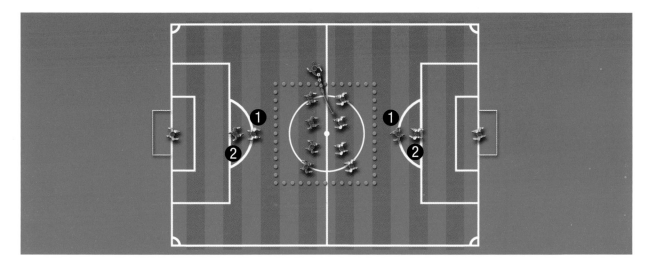

THE DRILL

• The coach starts the drill by feeding the ball to one team (whites in the diagram). The four opposition players (reds) in the marked-off area try to win the ball. The whites, meanwhile, try to complete three consecutive passes after which they can pass to their striker player 1 and "break out."

• If they are successful in completing three uninterrupted passes, two white players can break out of the marked area and only one opposition player can likewise leave the area to help defend against the attacking break. This will create a 3 vs. 2 situation. Employing speed and accuracy, the whites support their striker player 1 and attempt to create a goal-scoring opportunity.

• If, during the passing sequence, the reds win the ball, they can break immediately with a pass to their striker 1 and create their own 3 vs. 2 situation, going on to make an attempt on goal. Note, the same rules apply if the reds win the ball, i.e. just two attacking players and one defending player can break out of the marked area.

• Next time the coach gives the ball to the red team and it's their turn to try and complete three passes before they are allowed to break out. Whites now attempt to win the ball and can, of course, break if they succeed in disrupting the reds' passing.

COACHING POINTS

Here speed of movement and accuracy of passing are the keys to a successful drill. The forward-positioned strikers on both sides must be good at receiving and holding up the ball.

This is a demanding drill and you should rest the players from time to time.

4

GOALKEEPING—
THE BASICS

The art of successful goalkeeping is reliant on having sound technique, quick and efficient decision making, possession of positional sense and speed of movement. The goalkeeper is often the most isolated player on the field and often under the most pressure. While one mistake by a goalkeeper can lose a game (not something many outfield players will experience), one great save can keep his side in a match. Having the courage of his convictions and not being afraid to make a positive decision are key attributes.

Having natural ability and agility is essential, but these need to be combined with well-coached technique, honed by challenging match experiences. Goalkeepers more than any other position invariably improve with age. Peter Shilton, England's record-breaking goalkeeper, was still playing League football after his fortieth birthday, and this is not atypical; it is increasingly common for top-level soccer to employ goalkeepers well into their thirties.

Good players do not become great players without a wholehearted commitment to improving their game, and in this next section I have prepared a set of exercises and drills to sharpen most of the skills of the goalkeeper's craft.

BASIC HANDLING

Most of a goalkeeper's work involves the use of his hands, so good basic handling skills are essential. In this section we will cover the pick-up (scooping the ball from the ground and into the body), dealing with the direct shot into the body and shots above the head.

DRILL 81 The pick-up

PREPARATION The players stand facing each other 11 yards (10m) apart with a ball in the hands of the outfield player.

PLAYERS Two goalkeepers or a goalkeeper and an outfield player.

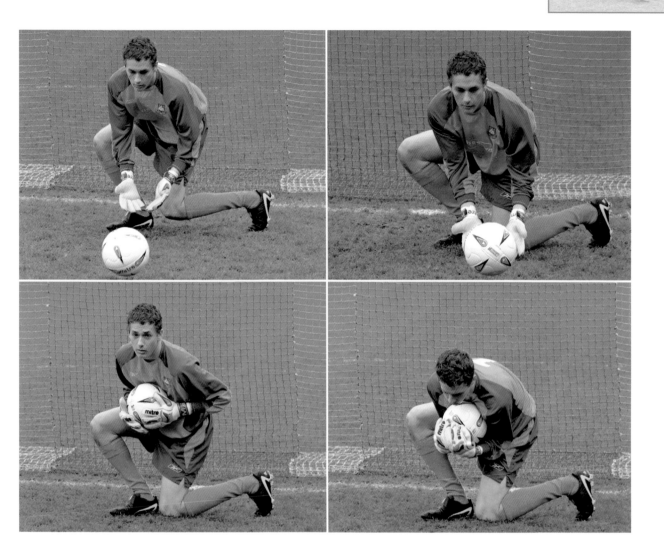

THE DRILL

• The first player rolls the ball along the ground to his partner and vice versa if two goalkeepers are paired up. Two basic techniques are used to collect and hold the ball, and either would be used in a match situation when the goalkeeper has time to get his whole body behind the ball.

COACHING POINTS

Technique 1 (shown on the left)

As the ball is rolled in, the goalkeeper gets his body in line with the ball, making sure that his feet are more or less together so the ball cannot go through them, and with the palms of his hands facing outward gathers the ball into his body using a scooping motion. His eyes must be on the ball all of the time.

As the goalkeeper's confidence grows, we increase the speed of delivery of the ball and start to roll balls to the side so he has to move his feet to get his body behind the ball.

Technique 2—using a bent knee (shown above)

As the ball is rolled toward the goalkeeper, his lower body and feet should be slightly sideways to the ball and the knee of the kneeling leg is just inside the heel of his other leg. With palms facing outward, the ball is scooped into the body. Again, increase the speed of the rolled ball as the players gain confidence.

DRILL 82 The direct shot into the body

PREPARATION Either work your goalkeepers in pairs or use an outfield player as a server. During the drill it is preferable to use a goal with one goalkeeper practicing while the other one serves. The quality of service to the performing player is vital, so don't underestimate the importance of your players practicing serving technique.

The performing goalkeeper must always be in a position of readiness: in a good balanced position; feet shoulder-width apart with his weight on the soles of the feet; hands at waist height and palms facing each other.

THE DRILL

• When first undertaking this drill, the server throws the ball into the goalkeeper below head height. Later, as confidence and technique improve, the server may progress to volleying the ball.

• The goalkeeper's action is to cup the ball into the body, relaxing the chest or waist on impact. The upper body folds over the ball when the ball is secure in the arms. The server should move his position from time to time, providing a fresh angle for the goalkeeper.

DRILL 83 Shots above the head

PREPARATION The set-up is the same as in the previous drill.

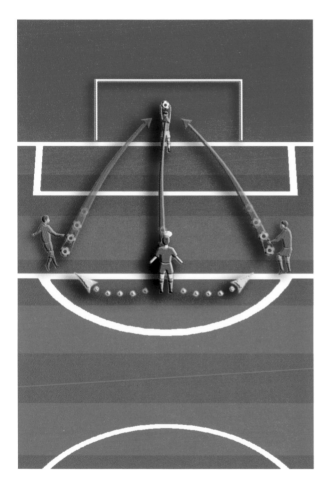

THE DRILL

• The server throws the ball toward the goal above the goalkeeper's head for him to catch. Later, when both the server's and goalkeeper's techniques permit, the server can add power and realism by volleying or chipping the ball toward the goal.

COACHING POINTS

When the goalkeeper catches the ball his hands and fingers should not be too rigid and the thumbs should be close together behind the ball. The hands should make a "W" formation behind the ball.

If the player needs to jump for the ball, then he must ensure that he takes off from one foot and not from a standing position using both feet.

Once the ball is caught, it must be secured into the body. Throughout the performance of the technique the head should be still and the eyes kept on the ball.

Alternate the positions of the server to make the goalkeeper adjust his position.

DRILL 84 Dealing with crosses—to catch or punch

PREPARATION   Use the area around the penalty box of a full-sized field.

PLAYERS   Two servers and one goalkeeper.

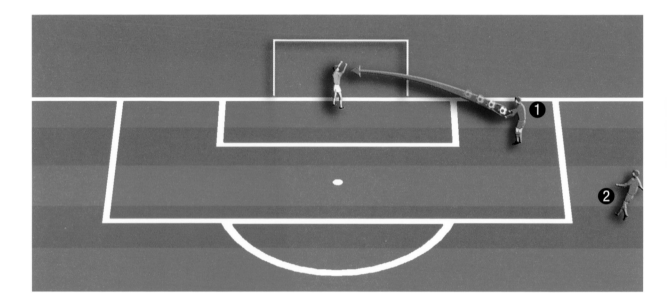

THE DRILL

• At its most basic level, player 1 will start the drill by throwing the ball into the six-yard box to simulate a crossed ball. When the goalkeeper is confident and showing good technique, the ball can be crossed by kicking from the position occupied by player 2 in the diagram.

COACHING POINTS

While this is the simplest of drills, there are a number of critically important technical elements that both the goalkeeper and the coach should keep in mind as it is performed: (1) The goalkeeper must adopt a good starting position; he should be about 1 yard (1m) off his line and in the center of the goal facing the ball with his body in an open stance; (2) he must judge the flight of the ball and make an early decision; (3) communicate positively with his defenders. Once the goalkeeper has made his decision to come for the ball he must tell his defenders. In opposed practice or match play, he must shout "keeper's ball" if he is dealing with the cross or

"away" when he wants his defenders to deal with the cross. Even in unopposed practice the coach should encourage the goalkeeper to communicate.

Once the goalkeeper has decided to come for the cross, he should move to take it at the earliest and highest point. If the goalkeeper hesitates you can be sure the attacking forwards will not, and may well beat him to the ball.

He should make a one-footed takeoff, bending the other leg and bringing his knee up. This helps with his elevation and will give some measure of protection from oncoming forwards.

The goalkeeper should try to catch the ball with slightly bent arms just in front of his body and above his head, which will allow him to see the ball into his hands. Once caught, the ball should be quickly brought into the body for protection.

DRILL 85 Dealing with crosses—using defenders and attackers

PREPARATION Use the area around the penalty box of a full-sized field.

PLAYERS You will need five players plus the goalkeepers. In the diagram the red team act as attackers and the white player is the sole defender. We use two forwards against one defender so that the goalkeeper is regularly brought into the action.

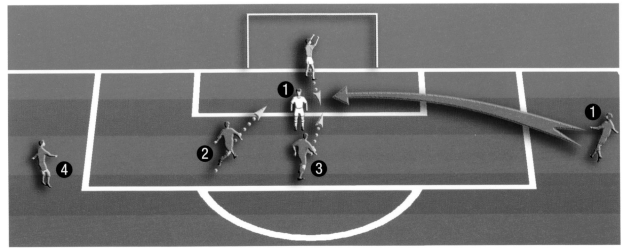

THE DRILL

• Attacking player 1 crosses the ball into the box for red players 2 and 3 to attack. As the cross is made the goalkeeper must utilize the three basic techniques outlined in the previous drill, i.e. he adopts a good starting position, quickly assesses the flight of the cross and, having made his decision, communicates it to his defenders.

• Now that he has defenders and forwards to consider, the goalkeeper has only a split second to evaluate his options—to catch, punch or deflect the ball away. If he elects to punch, his position and actions are similar to making a catch; he should try to punch two-fisted using the flat part of his fists, punching through the bottom half of the ball to help get distance. He should not swing the arms, but jab—keeping the hands together and the wrists firm. Occasionally, when under pressure or when the ball is moving away, a one-fisted punch is necessary: it's a more risky method, but is sometimes unavoidable.

DISTRIBUTION SKILLS

While it is widely understood that the goalkeeper is the last line of defense, it is sometimes forgotten that he is the initiator of many attacks on the goal.

Possession of the ball is the basic requirement of all controlled passing movements toward the goal by the attacking team, and there is nothing so frustrating as a goalkeeper making a fine save only to give up possession with a sloppy throw or wild kick. A goalkeeper's distribution should never put his own team under pressure nor cause an immediate threat to his own goal. And his distribution should be the first pass of his team's next attacking movement.

The following drills should help eradicate any weaknesses in your goalkeeper's distribution skills.

DRILL 86 Two-touch distribution with the feet

PREPARATION
Mark out an area of 66 x 22 yards (60 x 20m) into three zones.

PLAYERS
You will need seven outfield players and two goalkeepers.

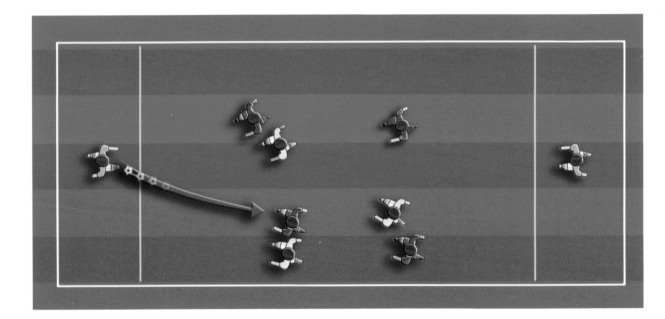

THE DRILL

• The drill starts with a 3 vs. 3 possession game with a floating seventh player making it a 4 vs. 3.

• The middle players maintain possession, occasionally passing back to either goalkeeper for him to control and pass back to the same team who passed him the ball. When the ball is with the goalkeeper the middle players must help him by making good passing angles. If the goalkeeper feels all the players are too close, he can pass directly to the goalkeeper at the opposite end.

• The goalkeepers cannot be challenged.

• This drill will make the goalkeeper more comfortable with the ball and give him confidence to take into match play.

DRILL 87 One-touch distribution with the feet

PREPARATION Mark out an area of 55 x 22 yards (50 x 20m). If you can additionally mark the area up into 11 yards (10m) grids it will help, but is by no means necessary.

PLAYERS You will need at least four outfield players and two goalkeepers.

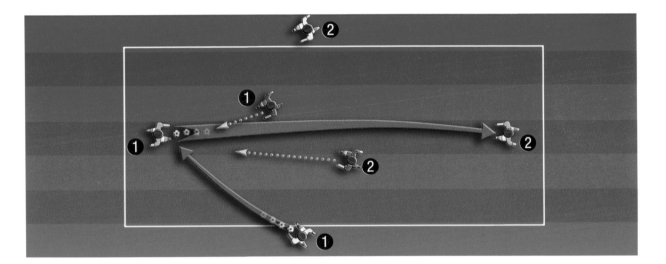

THE DRILL

• Server 1 passes the ball along the ground to goalkeeper 1. As soon as he receives the ball he must pass it back first time to either servers 1 or 2 or kick through the ball to goalkeeper 2. The drill is then repeated starting with server 2 passing to goalkeeper 2. Players 1 and 2, who must be at least 22 yards (20m) from the goalkeeper as the drill is restarted, try to block the pass from the goalkeepers.

• Occasionally change red 1 and 2 with white 1 and 2 as they tire.

COACHING POINTS

Server 1's pass along the ground to the goalkeeper simulates a back pass, and he must get in line with the ball as it is served in. If the goalkeeper now chooses to pass the ball long to the goalkeeper at the opposite end, he must get height and distance on his pass; if he is passing short back to either of the servers he should use the inside of his foot,

making firm contact. You can allow the goalkeeper two touches of the ball if it is obvious that they need it.

A goalkeeper who cannot deal with a back pass is a mistake waiting to happen and will badly undermine the confidence of his team.

In a match he will have to deal with back passes when he has plenty of time or is under pressure. If he has time he should take a controlling touch, bringing the ball under his control, which will result in a more accurate distribution.

If his time to deal with the back pass is compromised by the pressure of the opposition, then the keeper should elect to make a one-touch clearance. He is less likely to be accurate in reaching a teammate, but should avert a potentially dangerous situation. It is important that the goalkeeper practice both situations using both feet.

DRILL 88 The overarm throw

The overarm throw can be a potent attacking weapon, taking several opposition players out of the game when used at the right moment and performed well. It allows the goalkeeper to cover accurately a distance that would otherwise require a kick, and is usually used when the opposition has committed numbers in attack. A goalkeeper's overarm throw should be quick, accurate and help launch a counterattack.

The ball is held in the palm of the hand with the fingers spread, giving control and some manipulation of the ball. The throw is a bowling action delivered with a straight arm with the body slightly sideways; the non-throwing arm points in the direction of the target and acts as a counterbalance.

PREPARATION The drill is carried out on half of a full-sized field. You will need to put a goal on the halfway line.

PLAYERS Two goalkeepers and two outfield players.

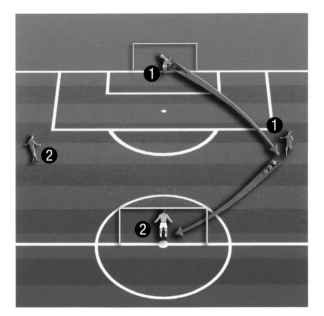

THE DRILL

• The outfield players are positioned facing goalkeeper 1, approximately halfway between the two goals and 11 yards (10m) to the right of the respective penalty areas.

• Goalkeeper 1 throws the ball overarm to the feet of player 1, who controls the ball and chips or drives the

ball to goalkeeper 2. He now repeats the sequence through player 2. It is important that the drill is performed in both directions—clockwise and counterclockwise.

• To speed things up the coach can set the condition that the goalkeepers must perform the throw within three seconds of catching the ball.

DRILL 89 Throwing the ball underarm

The ball is held in the palm, and with one foot planted in front of the other the ball is released along the ground from level with the front foot. The action is similar to that of tenpin bowling.

The underarm throw is used for short passes to players just outside the penalty area, about 22 yards (20m) away. It is important that the throw does not give the receiver any problems as he controls the ball.

PREPARATION   The three outfield players should be about 22 yards (20m) from the goalkeeper, facing him in a line, separated by approximately 16.5 yards (15m). You will need two balls.

PLAYERS   The drill requires one goalkeeper and three outfield players.

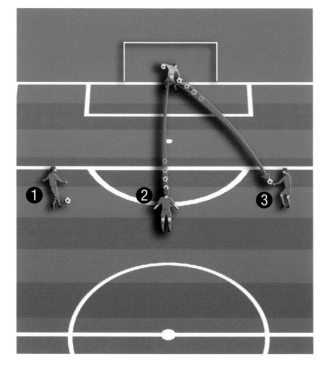

THE DRILL

• Players 1 and 2 start with balls at their feet. Player 2 delivers the ball to the goalkeeper, who catches and immediately rolls it to the "spare player" 3, who is on his far left.

• As the goalkeeper releases his throw, player 1 delivers his ball to the goalkeeper, who now rolls the ball to "spare player" 2, who is in the middle. The drill is continuous.

COACHING POINT

The goalkeeper works for approximately one and a half minutes, then rests before the drill is started again or if you have two goalkeepers, swap over. The throw must be controllable by the receiving players. Slow it down or speed it up depending on the skill level of the goalkeepers and players. The service from the outfield players must be accurate and may have to be varied and slowed. The goalkeeper must be working!

DIVING

Eye-catching, goal-stopping dives are what attracts young players to the position of goalkeeper in the first place; although great goalkeepers make it look easy, diving for the ball is a choice a goalkeeper makes based on experience and sound technique. A dive means the goalkeeper has insufficient time to move his feet and get his body in line with the shot: a good goalkeeper doesn't dive just to look spectacular.

High shots

Before diving for the ball the goalkeeper must try to adopt a well-balanced stance and be as still as possible. A dive for high shots away from the body begins with the weight on the foot nearest the ball followed by a push off on this leg. The hands should be close together, both reaching for the ball. If the goalkeeper elects to catch the ball, his fingers should be spread with thumbs together behind the ball. If the ball cannot be caught it should be parried away to safety—as far from the goal as possible and preferably out of bounds.

The goalkeeper completes the dive by landing on his side and shoulder, not his elbows, and if he catches the ball he should protect it by bringing it into his body as quickly as possible. Younger players have a tendency to favor one side when diving; the coach should watch for this and encourage practice on the weaker side.

The picture below shows a young goalkeeper at full stretch, diving to his right, but his timing is a little too late and the shot, which is high and accurate, evades him. Credit sometimes has to be given to the striker!

Low shots close to the body

The technique here is somewhat different than that used for high shots and is more difficult to master. For a low ball that is heading past the goalkeeper he must collapse his feet and get down quickly, leading with his hands because they will reach the ball before his body can.

One hand should be placed on top of the ball and the other behind it, and then the ball is pulled into the body.

Again the landing should be soft and on the shoulders and side, not the elbows, otherwise the ball can be jarred out of the hands.

DRILL 90 Diving—low shots close to the body

PREPARATION You will need an area approximately 11 x 16.5 yards (10 x 15m). Set up two "goals" using poles (or cones) 6.5 yards (6m) apart.

PLAYERS Two goalkeepers.

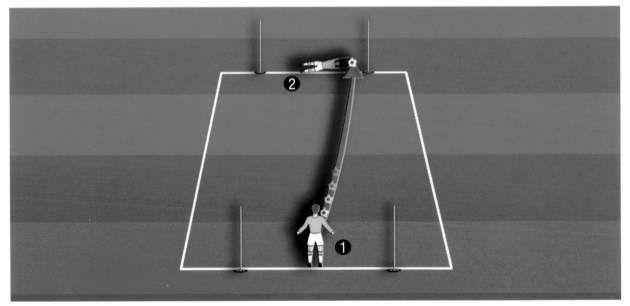

THE DRILL

• Goalkeeper 1 drops the ball from his hand and drives it, using the half-volley technique (see page 43), to goalkeeper 2, ensuring that the "shot" is reasonably close to the saving keeper and is along the ground.

• Goalkeeper 2 "reads" the shot and using the technique described on page 111, collapses his legs, leads with

both hands (keeping them in front of his body), lands on his shoulder and side and completes the save by pulling the ball into the body. The goalkeeper must not start his dive too soon, but read the direction and pace of the ball: it's almost impossible to change direction mid-dive.

• As confidence and skill levels improve, the ball can be driven harder and from a greater distance.

DRILL 91 Diving—high shots

PREPARATION The drill is carried out in the penalty box of a full-sized field.

PLAYERS Two players to act as servers plus the goalkeepers.

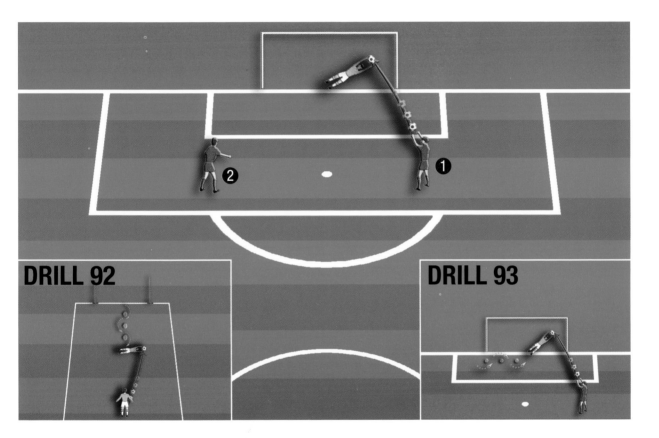

DRILL 92

DRILL 93

THE DRILL

• Player 1 throws the ball high to the goalkeeper's left. The goalkeeper, starting from a well-balanced position, dives to his left to make the "save." Once the keeper has recovered his position and is in the start position, player 2 repeats the drill, this time throwing the ball to the goalkeeper's right.

• As the goalkeeper's confidence grows and the correct technique is established, the difficulty of the drill is increased as players 1 and 2 step back to the edge of the penalty box and volley from their hands to the goalkeeper's right and left.

COACHING POINTS

Once the basic techniques of diving are mastered and the coach is satisfied that his goalkeepers are comfortable diving to both sides, the next stage is to introduce movement—backward and forward and along the goal line.

Set up the cones as shown in the inset diagrams above (drills 92 and 93) and insist that the goalkeeper weave in and out of all of the cones before making his saving dive. It is important that he uses small, shuffling steps and never crosses his feet over as he moves to the ball.

POSITIONING—NARROWING THE ANGLES

Talk to any experienced goalkeeper and they will tell you that if you master the art of positioning, everything else about the goalkeeper's craft follows easily.

Goalkeepers must combine two basic movements—moving into line with the ball and also moving forward toward the ball.

This will result in him "narrowing the angle" or effectively reducing the size of the target for a goal-approaching striker. Effective goalkeepers instinctively and quickly narrow the angle by smoothly moving into line and toward the ball in one movement.

A goalkeeper will be constantly adjusting his position in relation to the ball, even when it is in the opponent's half, at which time he should be on the edge of his penalty area on a line between the ball and his goal. This will keep him in touch with his defenders and in a position to react to the quick ball that penetrates his team's defense.

When the ball is in and around the penalty area it is important that he doesn't come too far forward, otherwise he risks being chipped. He should adopt a balanced, stationary stance as the shot is struck: it is extremely difficult to dive sideways when moving forward.

DRILL 94 Basic positioning 1

PREPARATION   The drill is carried out in the penalty area of a full-sized field.

PLAYERS   Goalkeeper and three outfield players.

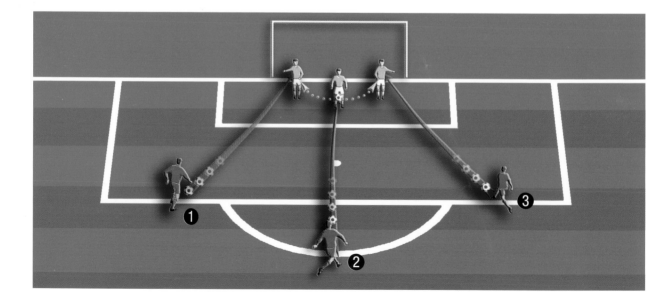

THE DRILL

• The three outfield players take it in turn to shoot at the goal once the goalkeeper has moved into the correct position in relation to the ball and after the coach is satisfied with his position.

COACHING POINTS

Ideally, the coach observes the goalkeeper's positional play from behind the goal, but standing behind the shooting players 1, 2 and 3 is also acceptable.

When the ball is with the central player 2, the goalkeeper

should be a few yards or meters off his line and in the center of the goal. As player 2 shoots, the goalkeeper should not be moving forward but be in a balanced stationary stance, which is his ready position.

As the ball is moved wide to player 3, the keeper must move quickly and smoothly across the goal to get in line with the ball, being careful not to show too much of the goal on left side.

When the ball is around the penalty area the goalkeeper must always anticipate a shot on goal.

DRILL 95 Basic positioning 2

PREPARATION The drill is carried out in the penalty area of a full-sized field.

PLAYERS Goalkeeper and three outfield players.

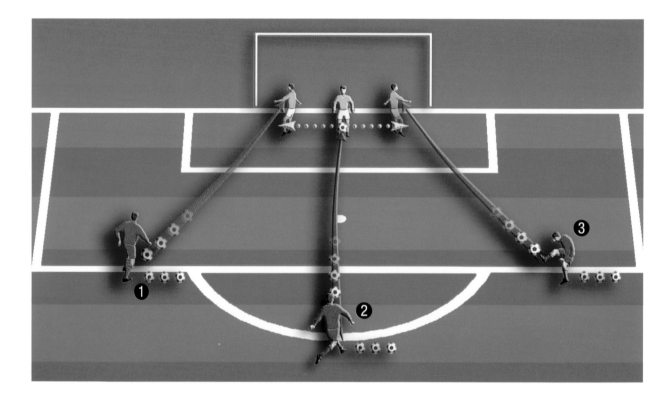

THE DRILL

• The previous drill can be developed by giving each outfield player three balls and asking them to shoot at the goal on the command of the coach, requiring the goalkeeper to adjust his position quickly.

• To begin with the coach asks them to shoot in sequence across the penalty area. This gives the goalkeeper time to adjust his position and get set for the shot. The command to shoot can be speeded up or slowed down, or even called randomly, according to the ability and performance of the goalkeeper.

• Alternatively, you can give the outfield players just one ball, which they pass across the penalty area,

making the goalkeeper adjust his position at every pass. After each player has touched the ball twice, shots are taken at random to test the goalkeeper's position and readiness.

• This in turn can be developed so that player 1 passes to player 2, who then must take three touches to score as the goalkeeper comes out to narrow the angle in what amounts to a realistic 1 vs. 1 situation.

• After the shot at the goal, the ball is given to player 3, who passes it to player 1, who repeats the drill; finally the ball is given to player 2, who has returned to his central position. He passes to player 3, who takes his three touches and attempts to score.

QUICK HANDS AND REACTIONS

An individual's speed of reaction is largely determined by their physical make-up and genes, but here are two drills that will improve the application of a goalkeeper's innate ability.

DRILL 96 Quick hands

PLAYERS   Two goalkeepers standing close together with a ball.

THE DRILL

• The first goalkeeper holds the ball with two hands below the hands of his partner, as shown in the pictures. He drops the ball and his partner must try to catch it before it hits the ground. This simple drill demands plenty of concentration and quick hands.

DRILL 97 Quick reactions

PLAYERS   Two goalkeepers standing 10 yards (6–8m) apart with a ball each.

THE DRILL

• The first goalkeeper, on the left, throws his ball high into the air above his own head.

• Simultaneously, the second goalkeeper throws his ball to the first goalkeeper, who must catch and return it to his partner before his own ball drops below a height at which he is able to catch it.

• In other words, the first or performing goalkeeper has to coordinate throwing and catching two balls, which will require a good deal of concentration and quick reactions.

COACHING POINTS

For more experienced goalkeepers, the distance between the pairs can be increased to 11–14 yards (10–12m) and the ball should be volleyed, rather than thrown, by the non-performing keeper.

Players should swap roles after six attempts.

DRILL 98 React and dive

PREPARATION The drill is set up in the penalty area of a full-sized field. A pole is placed halfway along the goal line about half a yard (half a meter) inside the goal, dividing the goal in two. You will need six balls for six tries.

PLAYERS Two goalkeepers.

THE DRILL

• Goalkeeper 1 stands at the near post, side on to his partner, facing toward the corner flag. Goalkeeper 2 stands 11 yards (10m) from the goal and to the left of the penalty spot, holding the ball (as shown in the diagram).

• Goalkeeper 2 shouts "now" and throws the ball toward the goal in the air, aiming for just inside the middle "post." Goalkeeper 1, on hearing the call, must react and save the "shot."

• Goalkeeper 1 makes six attempts to save the "shots" on the right side of the goal and then the players swap over. When both keepers have had six goes on the right, they move over and repeat the drill using the left half of the goal.

COACHING POINTS

The drill can be adjusted for more senior and experienced goalkeepers by moving the serving player back by a couple of yards (meters) and having him volley, rather than throw, the ball at the goal.

DRILL 99 React to save

PREPARATION
The drill is set up in the penalty area of a full-sized field. A pole is placed halfway along the goal line about half a yard (half a meter) inside the goal—dividing the goal in two. You will need six balls for six tries.

PLAYERS
Two goalkeepers and two outfield players.

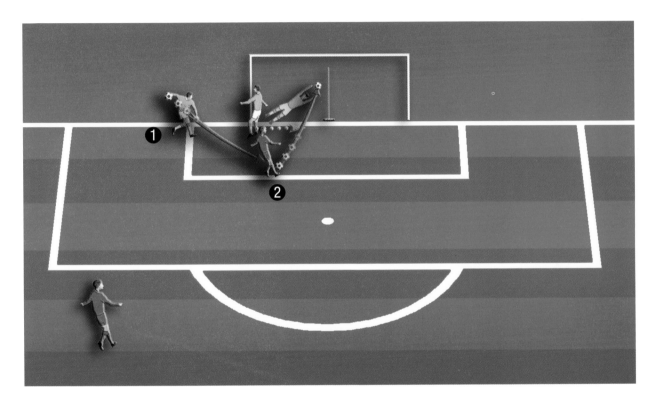

THE DRILL
• The performing goalkeeper stands at the near post, facing the second goalkeeper, designated player number 1 in this drill, who is holding the ball.

• Goalkeeper 1 throws the ball underarm, to the feet of player 2, who is stood on the six-yard line and who volleys the ball with the side of his foot (looking to place the shot) to the left and just inside the center pole.

• As soon as goalkeeper 1 has thrown the ball, the performing goalkeeper turns to face player 2 and attempts to save his shot.

• After six attempts at saving the shots, repeat the drill on the other side of the goal. Swap players after the drill has been completed on each side of the goal.

COACHING POINTS
The goalkeeper must constantly watch the ball, move quickly when he has assessed the flight and pace of it, never cross his feet as he moves across the goalmouth and push off with the left foot to dive to his left (and vice versa).

Quick reactions by the performing goalkeeper are as vital as they would be in a match situation.

5

SET PLAYS

Organization at set plays is everything, even for the most inexperienced of teams, and it should all begin on the training field with every player learning what is required of them: who is going to take the kick; who will make what runs; who is marking whom, and so on.

Set plays are the only moments during a game when a side can take the time they need to organize their attacking and defending strategies, and as a team it is important that both defending and attacking situations are regularly practiced. Great rewards (or disasters averted) can be realized as long as players are fully rehearsed and take up their positions and responsibilities the moment a set play is awarded.

In this section I have given you the basic setups for defending or attacking corners and organizing free kicks.

SETUP 1 Basic marking positions for defending a corner

In the diagram, the defending players (white) are set up to mark the attacking opposition (red), who are on the point of taking a corner from the left.

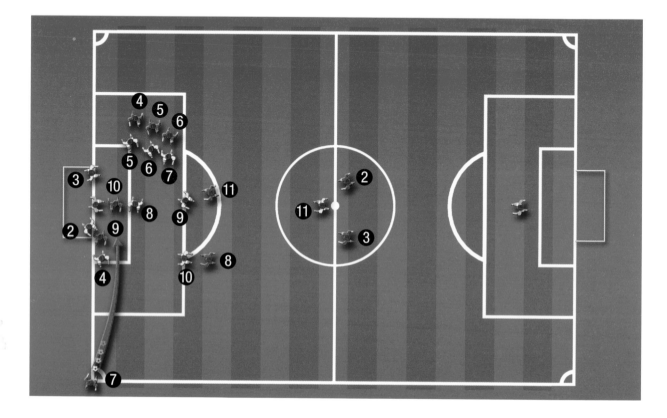

THE SETUP

• Red player 7 is preparing to take the corner with his right foot, which should make the ball swing in toward the goal. The attacking team has lined up as follows: player 9 on the near post; 10 in front of the goalkeeper; 4, 5 and 6 are positioned toward the far post and are ready to make runs to attack the ball; 11 and 8 are on the edge of the penalty area; and 2 and 3 are back defending any quick break from the white team.

• The defensive setup is as follows: player 4 is marking in front of red 9 to stop red 9 flicking the ball on; 2 and 3 are marking inside the posts; the goalkeeper takes up a position in the center of the goal; 8 is marking space centrally, but also making sure he is in front of red 10 to

stop red 10 having an unchallenged attempt on the goal. Players 5, 6 and 7 are the main markers and will generally be the best headers of the ball in the team. They must make sure they are in front of the players they are marking (red 4, 5 and 6), and keep both them and the ball in sight.

• Players 9 and 10 mark red 11 and 8 on the edge of the box and white 11 is left up field, hoping to spring a quick counterattack.

• Once the players have learned their starting positions and the setup has been well rehearsed, then the most important thing is being first to the ball when the corner is taken.

SETUP 2   Basic setup for an attacking corner

A successful corner kick is the product of two combined elements: the quality of the delivery of the ball and the timing of the runs that meet and attack it. Here are the attacking setups for two types of corners: the first is a basic setup and the second, on the next page, gives the opposition an additional problem to deal with.

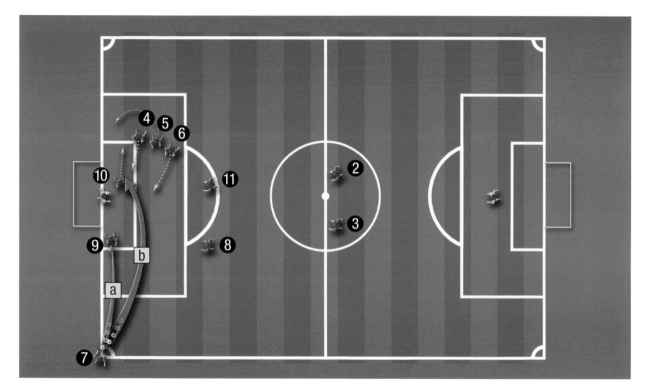

THE SETUP

• Player 7 is about to take the kick right-footed, and has two options available: (a) to try to chip the ball on to the head of his teammate 9, on the near post, who in turn flicks it on toward the onrushing attackers, or (b) to put more pace on the ball and swing it in toward the far post for his teammates to attack.

• The corner taker signals his intentions by either raising one hand in the air for option (a) or two hands in the air for option (b).

• In practice actual signals and their meaning are a closely guarded team secret, but you get the idea.

• When player 9 at the near post sees the signal, he either sets himself to head the ball on or, if 7 raises both hands, spins around to face his teammates, ready to attack any balls that drop back in the near-post area.

• Player 10 starts in front of the goalkeeper and, as the ball is delivered, pulls away to the far post (hoping to free himself of any marker). The timing of the runs of 4, 5 and 6 are critical. Option (a) requires that they fractionally delay their runs, or in the case of (b) make their runs more urgently. In the case of (b) I suggest 4 and 6 make direct runs to attack the ball with 5 spinning out and running toward the far post, hoping his movement will cause him to lose his marker. Timing is everything!

SETUP 3 Alternative attacking corner

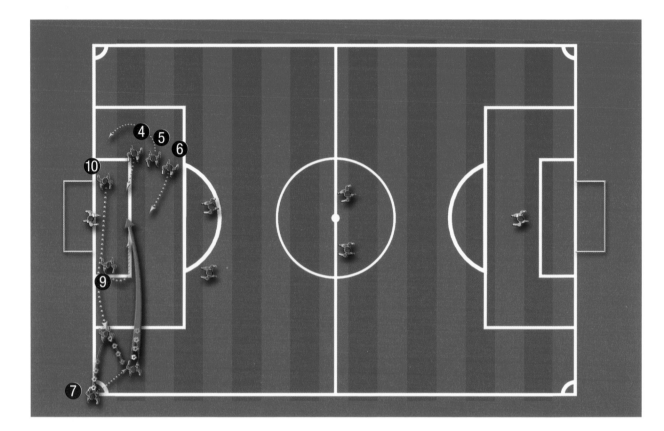

THE SETUP

• The players take up the same positions as in the previous setup, but this time the corner taker briefly holds the ball in the air with two hands before placing it on the ground.

• This tells his teammates what's coming and instructs player 9 to come short for the ball along the goal line. As player 9 gets just beyond the six-yard line, he turns and runs back toward the far post.

• Player 10, who is simultaneously moving along the goal line, now runs all the way toward the corner taker who, instead of taking the corner, passes the ball to his approaching teammate.

• Player 10 returns the ball to 7 who has, in the meantime, taken up a position approximately 11 yards (10m) from the corner flag. Player 7's angle on goal is now dangerous and threatening as he crosses the ball aiming for the far post. Player 10's pass back to 7 must have just the right pace so that he can cross with his first touch, surprising the opposition and giving them little or no time to react.

• Players 4, 5 and 6, who have likewise seen and interpreted 7's signal, must delay their runs to the eventual cross, which is swinging into the far post.

• The idea is that the movement of 9 and 10 and the different angle of the cross will cause uncertainty among the defenders and, by employing crisp speed of passing, good timing and an accurate final ball, give the attacking team a goal-scoring opportunity.

SETUP 4 An attacking free kick

The value of rehearsing set plays on the training field can never be underestimated. To start with, the basic positions and responsibilities of every player within the squad during dead ball situations must become second nature, and the movement around and off the ball, fake runs and, most importantly, the strike for goal be regularly practiced.

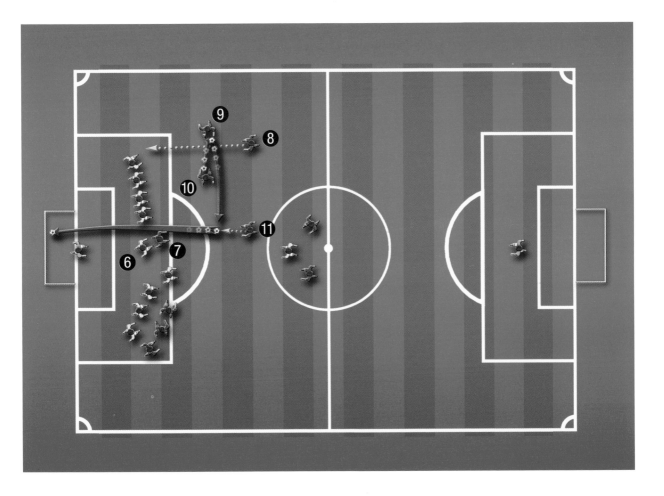

THE SETUP

• The diagram illustrates a free kick to be taken 22 yards (20m) from, and to the right of, the goal. Attacking player red 10 is poised and ready over the ball facing his teammate 9, who is 1 yard (1m) away.

• Player 10 passes the ball to 9, who stops it. Player 8 runs at the ball as if to strike it, but just before player 8 "strikes" the ball, player 9 passes it square to the

approaching 11, who shoots for the goal—probably with his left foot.

• With the right timing and disguise, the defending team can be completely tricked and player 11 should have a relatively clear sight of (and shot on) the goal.

• Red player 7 should try to block defender white 6 from closing the ball down as 11 shoots.

6

SOLVING PROBLEMS

I am sure that after most games, particularly when the team has lost, the coach reflects on how things have gone and tries to analyze the reasons why his team has performed the way it has.

Usually you learn more about your team in defeat, when reflections on the game and the assessment of individual players are not clouded by the euphoria of victory—something that can gloss over a multitude of performance sins!

This section of the book covers ten common team and coaching problems, and looking at the possible causes should help you pinpoint and address possible weaknesses in your team. I have tried to give you a range of solutions for each problem, linked to the drills, setups and advice in the book. It should all add up to a useful armory of coaching ideas that will go some way to assisting you organize productive training sessions that will aid your team's development.

Remember: don't make changes for change's sake, and when you do alter things, be as sure as you can that it will lead to an improvement in your team's performance. The players you drop this week may be the players you need next week if things don't get better!

The numbers shown here refer to the drill, the set play and the small-sided game number.
A full list of drills, set plays and small-sided games with their page numbers can be found on page 143.

PROBLEM 1 *The team gives too many goals away from crosses.*

POSSIBLE CAUSES

1   The fullbacks do not do enough to stop the crosses from the opponent's wide players.
2   The wingers let the opposition fullbacks get forward, allowing attacking 2 vs. 1 situations to arise.
3   The centerbacks do not attack the ball as it is crossed and are poor at marking.
4   The goalkeeper is staying on his line and not coming for the crosses.

SOLUTIONS

1   Work your fullbacks to improve closing down and jockeying (1 vs. 1).

	51	52	53

2   Educate your wingers to go with runners, which in this case are the opposition's fullbacks.

	42	52

3   Improve your centerbacks' starting positions and heading skills.

	31	32	33	34	49	50

4   Improve the goalkeeper's understanding of how to deal with crossed balls.

	69	84	85

PROBLEM 2 *The team doesn't score enough goals: the team doesn't shoot.*

POSSIBLE CAUSES

1   The team suffers from a lack of confidence in front of the goal.
2   The forwards lack technique when shooting.
3   The team does not get forward in numbers and the front players lack support, especially from midfield players.
4   The attacking play is not direct enough. The front players overelaborate and pass too often instead of shooting.

SOLUTIONS

1   Do you, as coach, criticize too much? Encourage your players more, make shooting practice sessions successful and make it clear that missing during training doesn't matter—just keep trying.

2   Practice kicking and shooting techniques every session and look at the makeup of your squad. Can you make changes?

	35	36	37	38
	58	59	🐥 2	3	4

3   Reemphasize team shape and responsibilities. Get the ball in to the front players quickly and make sure you have good width in attack. Push up from the back, which will push the players in front forward. Encourage the midfield to make forward runs.

	64	65	66	67	68	69	🐥 5

4   Do not overplay in the defensive and middle thirds of the field. Hit the front players with "the first ball out." Get crosses in early and shoot at every opportunity—players should not be afraid to miss.

	60	61	62	63	🐥 2	4	5

Key   📊 Drills   ⚽ Set Plays   🏐 Small-Sided Games

PROBLEM 3   *The team concedes too many goals from direct play.*

POSSIBLE CAUSES

1   Not organized defensively and lacks shape.
2   Defensively, the team lets balls bounce, giving the opposition the advantage.
3   The back line lacks pace and is slow to react to potentially dangerous situations.
4   Midfield and defenders let players run off them.

SOLUTIONS

1   Define responsibilities and get defenders to work as a unit. Play more compactly. ──────────▶ 📊 | 46 | 54

2   Improve starting positions and make sure your players attack the ball in the air or as it bounces. The team must be proactive rather than reactive. The team must defend first and you should demand a positive approach from them. But don't let them push up too high, leaving space in behind. ──────▶ 📊 | 39 | 40 | 49 | 50 | 54 | 🏐 | 5

3   Don't defend too high up the field. Make sure that the back line is together, push up as a unit and drop off as a unit. Don't let balls bounce and deny space in behind by dropping off early. ──────▶ 📊 | 53 | 54

4   Work the team on going with runners off the ball. Make sure the players understand and accept their responsibility to track runners—they must not mark too tight but "see the ball and the man." Don't let your players "ball watch." ──────────▶ 📊 | 41 | 42 | 🏐 | 6

PROBLEM 4   *The team doesn't score from set plays.*

POSSIBLE CAUSES

1   There is no planning, no set routines.
2   Delivery and execution are poor.
3   Nobody attacks the ball and there is a lack of movement when the ball is delivered.
4   Finishing is poor.

SOLUTIONS

1   Plan and practice. ──────────▶ ⚽ | 2 | 3 | 4

2   Practice delivery and kicking skills. ──────────▶ 📊 | 2 | 3

3   Be specific about who does what and rehearse on the training field. Make sure you pick the right players for the job. ──────▶ ⚽ | 2 | 3 | 4

4   Set up and practice possible game scenarios to improve technique. If necessary, isolate particular techniques, e.g. heading 1 vs. 1. ──────▶ 📊 | 55 | 56 | 57

PROBLEM 5 *The team concedes too easily from corners.*

POSSIBLE CAUSES

1 Poor organization and team roles have been insufficiently defined.
2 Players do not attack the ball and the defending is too static.
3 The goalkeeper does not always come for crosses.
4 The team is weak under challenges.

SOLUTIONS

1 Define starting positions for your players—who is marking the posts, the opposition's attackers or space? ⬤ 1

2 Look at the starting positions and improve the technical competence and confidence of the assigned players. Have you got the right players in the right positions? Emphasize being "first to the ball." 32 33 34 49 50

3 Look at the goalkeeper's starting position. Encourage him to come for the cross if there is enough height on the ball. Coach to improve his technique and confidence and the level and quality of communication with his defenders. 84 85 ⬤ 1

4 Look at your personnel: can you change them? Do your tall players mark the opposition's tall players, or is there a mismatch? Coach to improve technique and confidence and encourage his players to be proactive rather than reactive: this means, assuming their starting positions are correct, that players make the decision to attack the ball and are first to the ball. 43 44

PROBLEM 6 — *The goalkeeper does not come for crosses.*

POSSIBLE CAUSES

1 Lacks confidence when confronted with high balls.
2 Has poor technique.
3 Makes poor or no decisions.
4 Does not appear to be brave enough and, possibly, fears contact with other players.

SOLUTIONS

1 Spend time coaching your goalkeeper to improve his technique and build up his confidence. ————————————→ | 🧍 | 49 | 50 | 84 | 85 |

2 Practice when to punch and when to catch; when to come for the ball or when to stay on the line and practice opposed and unopposed during training. ————————————→ | 🧍 | 84 | 85 |

3 Rehearse match situations and encourage your goalkeeper to assess each crossed ball. Don't let him be afraid to make mistakes during practice. When he makes the decision to come for the ball, make sure he repeatedly comes all the way without hesitation. Successful outcomes on the training field will breed confidence. ————————————→ | 🧍 | 49 | 50 | 84 | 85 |

4 Use opposed practice to encourage decision-making and get him used to attackers and defenders in the penalty box. Reinforce the message that it is better to come for the ball and make a mistake than not to come at all. Age permitting, consider an upper-body strength conditioning program. ————————————→ | ⚽ | 1 | ✏️ | 4 |

PROBLEM 7 — *The team doesn't pass well enough.*

POSSIBLE CAUSES

1 Too many touches in possession and playing with the head down.
2 Players exhibit poor control, constantly losing possession.
3 Players play the "wrong pass" or play negatively—too many square or backward passes.
4 The team lacks movement and plays too slowly.

SOLUTIONS

1 Set conditions during drills and small-sided games—one, two or three touches. Get a "picture of play"—control, pass and move. ————————————→ | 🧍 | 9 | 10 | 11 | 12 | ✏️ | 1 |

2 Coach to improve technique, concentrating on the first touch. ——→ | 🧍 | 5 | 6 | 7 | 8 |

3 Make the "first pass" a forward pass and encourage the team to play forward as early as possible. ————————————→ | 🧍 | 3 | 12 | ✏️ | 5 |

4 Encourage your players to support the player on the ball and practice movement off the ball. Practice playing more quickly with one or two touches to help players time their runs. Teach that movement creates space and space means more time. ————————————→ | 🧍 | 11 | 12 | ✏️ | 1 | 5 |

PROBLEM 8 *The team lacks motivation.*

POSSIBLE CAUSES
1   There are too many "bosses"—who, exactly, is in charge?
2   Training sessions are too repetitive and boring.
3   Your team selection favors certain players.
4   The team's poor record is lowering morale and sapping enthusiasm.

SOLUTIONS
1   Make sure everybody knows. One boss, one voice! And set
    clear standards for discipline, time-keeping and so on. ⟶ | Introduction and Coach's Page |
2   Make training as varied and enjoyable as possible.
    This book should help!
3   Be fair or be seen to be fair—even if it means dropping your own children
    from the team one week! You will gain the other players' respect. Under
    no circumstances show favoritism to any individual.
4   Try not to be too critical when the team loses; instead emphasize to the
    players the team ethic of "win together, lose together." Winning is great,
    but it is not everything. Set targets, even goals against!

PROBLEM 9 *The opposition passes the ball through us too easily.*

POSSIBLE CAUSES
1   The team is too spaced out on the field.
2   No one is getting close enough to the opposition.
3   Players are not competing hard enough or tackling.
4   Players switch off when the team loses possession of the ball—"it's not our job to
    win it back."

SOLUTIONS
1   Reemphasize team shape and coach the team to be more compact
    when defending using attack vs. defending and conditioned
    practice games. ⟶ | 👤 | 46 | 54 | 🎽 | 5 |
2   Define responsibilities for every player—for example, the nearest player to
    the ball closes the ball down and the others respond: midfield
    marks midfield, wingers stop overlapping fullbacks,
    and so on. ⟶ | 👤 | 24 | 41 | 42 | 45 | 46 |
3   Coach to improve 1 vs. 1 defending and emphasize that it is everyone's
    responsibility to win the ball. Make this a team habit—something "we
    always do." Practice man-to-man marking and convince the
    team to become more competitive. ⟶ | 👤 | 47 | 48 | 49 | 🎽 | 6 |
4   The whole team defends, not just the defenders. It is part of the
    team ethic that we "always win the ball back as quickly as
    possible" and don't just play when "we have the ball." ⟶ | 👤 | 45 | 46 | 🎽 | 6 |

PROBLEM 10 *The team regularly loses in the last fifteen minutes.*

POSSIBLE CAUSES

1 Fatigue.
2 Dissipation of concentration levels—usually a symptom of fatigue.
3 Have you used your substitutes correctly?
4 The team lacks discipline and loses organization.

SOLUTIONS

1 Improve the fitness of the squad and study their hydration levels—are they taking in fluids at the right times and could you be guilty of over-training players? Take professional advice about conditioning and fitness programs for soccer players.

2 Poor hydration may be at the root of the problem again. Get players to take in fluids during breaks in play. Give players targets for the second half—for example, no goals to be scored by the opposition during set plays or "your player" doesn't score and so on. This should help improve concentration levels. ⟶ 6

3 Do you make your substitutions too quickly? Are you taking off and putting on the right players? Are your substitutions making the team's performance better or worse? Don't make too many positional changes when making substitutions.

4 Look at the players' behavior and performance during training. Ask yourself whether the signs are there: do they argue; give up; is there tension between certain players; are they sufficiently focused? Make sure the captain is a leader who can and does lead. What are the players doing the day before a match—are they getting enough rest? Make sure rules for behavior and discipline are clearly understood and everybody observes the ethic—"the team comes first." ⟶ 5 6

7

SMALL-SIDED GAMES

During the course of most training sessions the coach will, at some point, get the squad to play a small-sided game. A simple 7 vs. 7 or 8 vs. 8 is a fine way to finish off a day or evening's work, but sometimes it is a good idea to impose conditions on the game to emphasize a specific coaching point or reinforce a team tactic.

Small-sided or conditioned games are an excellent way for players to absorb fresh tactical or technical components of the game.

Here are six conditioned games that will make your players think about specific aspects of their game.

GAME 1   Below head height—3 vs. 3

By ruling out balls played over the head, players are encouraged to pass the ball among the team to penetrate the opposition: no direct soccerball with high, long passes forward.

This condition is particularly useful with young players, who are encouraged to support the player on the ball by making good passing angles; it also promotes movement off the ball.

PLAYING AREA   44 x 16.5 yards (40 x 15m) with a 5.5 yard (5m) "no-go zone" at each end complete with two small goals (poles or cones are fine, placed 1.5 yards (1.5m) apart.

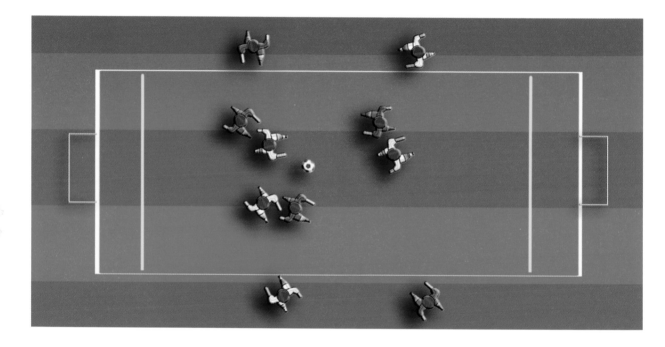

CONDITION

• The ball must remain below head height all of the time.

• When the side in possession offends by playing the ball too high, it immediately hands possession over to the opposition. Both teams try to score in the small goals at each end.

• Neither the attacking nor defending teams can enter the "no-go zones" at any time.

• You can introduce side players to produce wall passes, but limit them to a maximum of two touches.

COACHING POINTS

The game promotes passing between and around the opposition—not over them. It demands that the players off the ball make good passing angles, it encourages support and movement, and practices passing skills with quick interplay between teammates.

During the game you can also set additional conditions: for example two or three touch soccer for both teams.

GAME 2 One touch to finish

This encourages one-touch shooting and sharpens forward players' instincts around the goal. It also helps to improve the awareness of players on the ball who must pick out teammates in better scoring positions.

PLAYING AREA A 44 x 22 yards (40 x 20m) area for a game of 6 vs. 6 including goalkeepers.
The game can be expanded by adding players up to a maximum of 8 vs. 8 and increasing the area to 66 x 44 yards (60 x 40m).

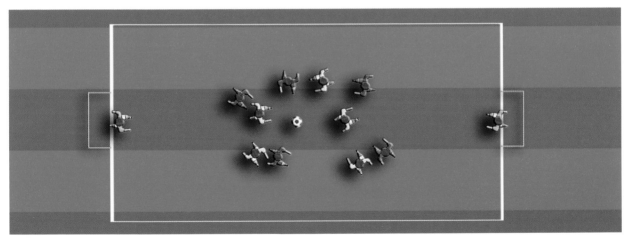

CONDITION

The condition imposed is that the player shooting or heading for the goal can only have one touch on the ball, i.e. he must perform a first-time shot or header.

COACHING POINTS

We have restricted the forwards to a first-time shot, and this should have the effect of sharpening their finishing skills and increasing the general awareness of players around the goal.

The players off the ball must anticipate possible goal-scoring opportunities and those taking possession of the ball, and who are not in a position to score with one touch, must learn to pick out teammates in scoring positions.

GAME 3 Rebounds to score

By forcing players to anticipate and react to a ball coming back into play from a rebound, we can discourage players off the ball from just watching and waiting. It makes non-shooting players follow up shots (mimicking a parried save from a goalkeeper) and stops defenders switching off, as they may have to clear the rebound.

PLAYING AREA
A sports hall, gymnasium or anywhere with goals that can be marked on a solid surface that will supply the rebounds. When you are outside you can use benches placed on their sides in the goalmouth.

The diagram shows a 7 vs. 7 game, played without goalkeepers, of course. Numbers can be adjusted for smaller sports halls or gyms.

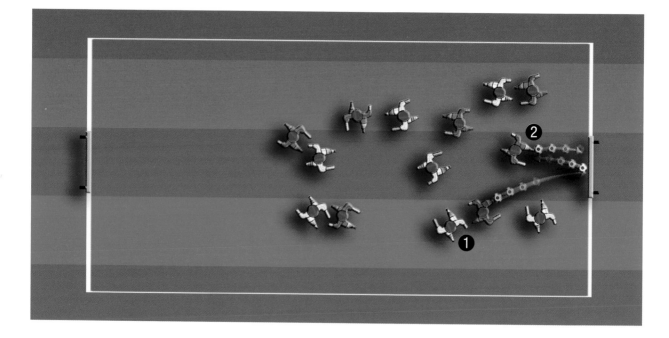

CONDITION

• The game is played normally, but to score a goal the following must happen: the first shot on the goal doesn't score; the ball will rebound off the wall (or bench) and must be struck into the goal again, with a maximum of two touches (three touches for very young players), to count.

• In the diagram red 1 shoots and hits the goal, red 2, following up, "scores" with his shot when the ball rebounds into his path.

COACHING POINTS

Since the striker can't "score" the first time, this game naturally encourages other players to get up and support the striker.

It forces teammates to follow up shots at the goal and improves their anticipation, making them think about where the ball will go. It will also stop defenders switching off because they will be regularly called upon to clear the rebounds.

GAME 4   Only score from a cross and finish

This game encourages width in the team, which may well be lacking. It is designed to improve crossing technique and encourages forwards to attack crosses. Defensively, the goalkeeper and the defending unit will have a lot of crosses to deal with.

PLAYING AREA Position two goals on the edge of each penalty area and mark off the wide areas (the width of the penalty area) with disks. Players 1 and 2 from each side are the only players allowed in the wide areas.

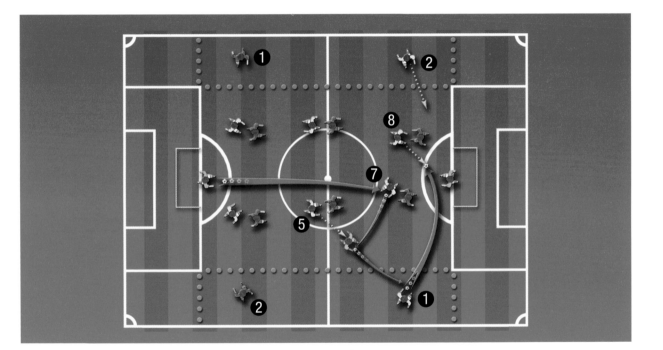

CONDITION

• A game of 7 vs. 7, including the two goalkeepers, is played in the central area of the field. A goal can only be scored when the attacking team's wide players (players 1 and 2) cross the ball and it is headed, shot or volleyed into the goal.

• In addition, the ball can only be passed to the wide players by the attacking team's midfield players or forwards, not their defenders or goalkeeper.

• In the diagram the goalkeeper throws to white 7, who has 5 in support, 7 passes to 5, who in turn pushes the ball out wide to 1. Player 1 now crosses the ball, which is attacked by 8.

• Finally, the opposite winger (white 2 in the diagram) is also allowed to come in and attack the cross.

COACHING POINT

By limiting scoring opportunities to balls crossed from wide positions, the game will naturally create width in the team. It teaches forwards to anticipate crosses and improves crossing technique. It also encourages wingers to get involved in attacking crosses at the far post.

GAME 5   One touch in own half

If you feel that your team's buildup play is too slow or your defenders are taking too many risks on the ball, then applying a condition that restricts players to one touch of the ball in their own half is a great way of making them deal more urgently with the ball at their feet. It may also help the team to stay more compact if they push up quickly out of the defensive third when defenders play forwards with an immediate one-touch pass.

PLAYING AREA   An area of 66 x 44 yards (60 x 40m) for a game of 8 vs. 8 including goalkeepers. The playing area size can be adjusted for smaller groups.

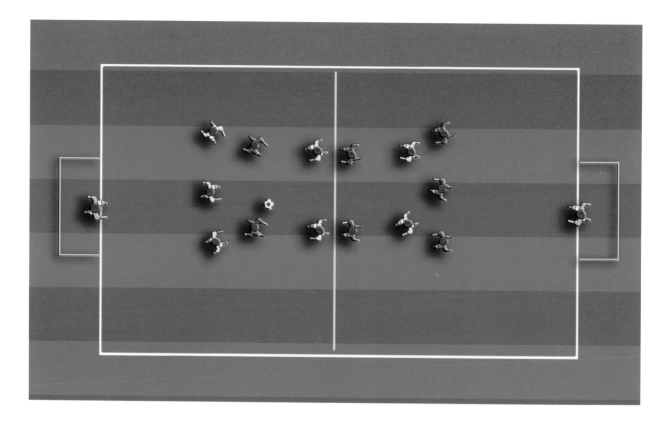

CONDITION

A normal game is played with the strict condition that every player, with the exception of the goalkeepers, is allowed only one touch of the ball in their defending half of the field. In the attacking half players play their usual game.

COACHING POINTS

The effect of the condition is to speed up attacking play and for defenders to clear danger quickly. It also stops overplay in the wrong areas and improves qualities of concentration and anticipation.
The team will tend to play more as a unit and will respond to the instruction "move up the field."

You should encourage your players to pass as accurately as possible during the build of attacks, not just kick and rush, or the ball will just keep coming back into their defensive half.

GAME 6 Man-to-man marking

This game is physically demanding, so in order to keep the quality of the play high you should introduce regular rest periods.

It can be adapted for individual players or for separate team units (e.g. just the midfielder or defenders).

The flip side of the man-to-man marking coin is the ability of marked players to shrug off or lose their markers; during the game a coach must stress to his players that they should use their individual talents and skills—to run with the ball, perform turns and to make runs off the ball—to lose their markers.

PLAYING AREA The diagram shows an area of 55 x 33 yards (50 x 30m) for a game of 6 vs. 6 including goalkeepers. The area can be adjusted for larger or smaller groups.

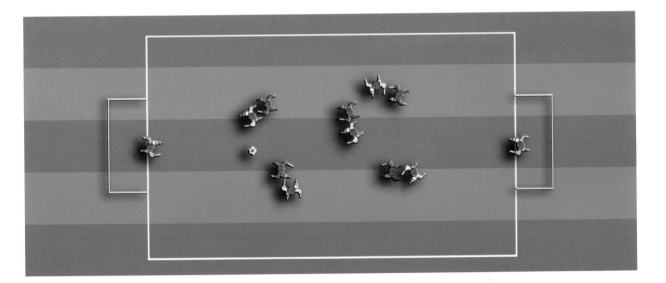

CONDITION

The game is played normally with no restrictions on touches, but at the outset every player is given an opposition player to mark and becomes the only player allowed to dispossess his nominated player of the ball. All outfield players are marking man-to-man.

COACHING POINTS

From the defensive point of view, the game will help perfect the qualities of both individuals and the team. It will sharpen defensive concentration and improve team discipline largely because "every player has a job to do" and must continually intercept balls to, and tackle his, nominated player.

The attacking team learns to play under pressure, and movement on and off the ball—aimed at losing markers—is practiced in a game situation. For attackers it encourages individuality, offering them a chance to repeatedly turn, perform stepovers, try fakes and changes of pace, dribble and use every other trick in their armory of ball skills.

THE COACH'S PAGE

As a youth coach my role focuses on refining players' technique. My job is to teach all of the game's basic skills, from control and passing to tackling and heading. It's so important to give the players in your care a solid grounding in basic technique when they are young; only by doing this will they be properly prepared for senior soccer.

As the players grow older, the coaching emphasis tends to shift toward the need for organization and better game understanding. I am aiming to produce good all-round, creative and intelligent players, well equipped for the team's requirements and the fast-paced, physical and highly skillful modern game.

Soccer is, at its heart, a simple game based on intelligent interpassing, and for younger players skills, technique and good movement are most easily grasped if the drills and practices are, in turn, kept simple. As a result many of the drills I use do not involve opposition. I want the players to learn to play a one- and two-touch passing game, only adding opposition when the players are comfortable and confident when receiving possession. You should be constantly encouraging the concept of pass and move.

The areas and dimensions for the drills throughout this book are accurate guidelines, but adjustments may have to be made. For younger, less experienced players you may need to give them larger areas in which to work, alternatively the more experienced players should be challenged with smaller and more testing areas.

Keeping possession of the ball is paramount, and every player needs to develop the skills and the desire to keep the ball because good passing combined with intelligent running off the ball means that players will create and exploit space, giving problems to the opposition and ultimately opening them up to create goal-scoring opportunities.

Coaching is hard work, and your effectiveness on the training field will only be as good as the time you spend on preparation beforehand. At West Ham we operate from a coaching syllabus and after every session the coaching staff always have to ask themselves, and answer honestly, the following questions. You should do likewise.

Was I planned and prepared for all sessions?

Did I communicate effectively?

Did the players understand my instructions?

Did I challenge the players enough and were the practices too easy or too hard?

Did the players learn something today?

What were my coaching behaviors?

How much praise, information and criticism did I deliver?

Did I coach all the players or just a select few?

And lastly, did they all enjoy it?

INDEX OF DRILLS

Author acknowledgments

I would like to offer sincere thanks to all of the following for their welcome help during the preparation of this book: the West Ham United Board of Directors for allowing the use of the stadium for the photographs; the Academy players of West Ham United F.C. for demonstrating their wonderful soccer skills and for their patience during the photo-shoot, especially Jack Jeffery! Reebok for supplying the training kit and Trevor Webb, Stan Burke and Doug Robertson for getting the field, kit and equipment organized.

Jonathan Hayden for his advice and professional approach while putting it all together.

The ever-patient and excellent photographer Paul Harding and designers Martin Barry and Kevin Tungate.

I would like to pay tribute to writer Adam Ward, who died tragically during the initial stages of preparing the book; a massive West Ham fan who is sadly missed.

Special thanks to Rio Ferdinand for his time and effort in penning the foreword—thanks Rio, it's much appreciated.

Finally, none of this would be possible without the continual support and encouragement of my family, Brenda, Dean, Neil and Louise.

Picture acknowledgments

All photography © **Octopus Publishing Group Limited**/Action Images except the following listed below:
© **Octopus Publishing Group Limited**/Jonathan Hayden pp. 4/5, 10, 16, 37, 43, 44, 45, 49, 66 (2 on right), 80, 91, 92, 108, 130, 133, 144
© FAOPL p. 6

Publisher's acknowledgments

Executive Editor: Trevor Davies
Executive Art Editor: Karen Sawyer
Design: Martin Barry and Kevin Tungate
Illustrations: Martin Barry
Production Controller: Martin Croshaw
Photography: Paul Harding at Action Images and Jonathan Hayden